THE
PIGEON COOK

J. C. Jeremy Hobson and Philip Watts

THE CROWOOD PRESS

First published in 2010 by
The Crowood Press Ltd
Ramsbury, Marlborough
Wiltshire SN8 2HR

www.crowood.com

British Library Cataloguing-in-Publication Data
A catalogue record for this book is available from the British Library.

ISBN 978 1 84797 228 6

Originated by The Manila Typesetting Company

Printed and bound in India by Replika Press

Contents

Acknowledgements

It is our experience that you only have to mention the fact that you are writing a pigeon cook book and you will be inundated with ideas and suggestions – a fact for which we are, of course, grateful, but not at all surprised as pigeons, both domestic and wild, have been an important source of food for many centuries.

Some of the recipes contained within these pages have been adapted by us: a few come from books that first saw the light of day in the late 1800s, and three or four have been taken from our book *Cook Game*, also published by The Crowood Press. The greater proportion have, however, been included in this book as a result purely and simply of the kindness shown to us by various chefs and cooks we have met on our culinary travels, and without whom it would have been impossible to compile. In addition to their recipes they have also shared their knowledge and given us many of those little tips and wrinkles that make all the difference in the kitchen.

In thanking everybody we hope we've done just that and not left anyone out: if we have, it is due entirely to inefficient note-keeping, for which we apologize in advance! We are most grateful to all those who gave us a bed and fed and watered us on our little road trips, and especially to the chefs we met whilst there. Our sincere thanks must therefore go to all at the Hoste Arms, Burnham Market, Norfolk – Paul Whittome (owner), Andrew McPherson (director) and Gemma Arnold (chef); to John Hoskins, owner of The Old Bridge, Huntingdon, his general manager Nina Beamond and to their head chef Simon Cadge; to Sir Thomas and Lady Ingilby, owners of the Boar's Head, Ripley, near Harrogate, North Yorkshire, their general manager Steve Chesnutt, and of course their head chef Kevin Kindland. Chris and Alison Davy looked after us well at the Rose and Crown, Romaldkirk, Co. Durham, as did Joanne Butler at The Bell, Horndon on the Hill, Essex. Chefs Stuart Fry and Stephen Treadwell run the kitchens at The Bell with quiet efficiency, and even though they were preparing for a busy Sunday lunchtime when we visited, could not have been more helpful with their time and experiences.

Others who gave of their time include James Rogers at The Dog at Grundisburgh, Suffolk, and Lawrence and Julia Murphy at Fat Olives, Emsworth, Hampshire. Janet Hutchings at The Bell at Skenfrith, Monmouthshire, was kind enough to offer not only a recipe, but also a photo of the dish – and very appetizing it looks, too! Sue Gibson of Macbeth's game dealers based in Moray, Scotland, gave us some good ideas, as did Alice Booth and Melinda Hobson.

Naomi Roberts is the PR and promotions executive at Bonner & Hindley Communications, Leeds; she did a brilliant job of organizing one particular 'road trip' on our behalf, and we are extremely grateful to her for doing so.

You cannot have a pigeon recipe book without including pigeon pie! We looked for one on the internet and came up with what we considered to be the best recipe, which happened to be featured on Gourmet Britain's website. When we wrote to him, Simon Scrutton was only too pleased to allow us to use it in *The Pigeon Cook* and we would like very much to thank him for this. As pickles and chutneys go so well with a lot of pigeon dishes, we have included just a few recipes from our book *Making Modern and Traditional Chutneys, Pickles and Relishes* (published by The Crowood Press in 2010), and would therefore like to thank Mary Hart and Lynn Brodie for allowing us to use them once more here.

Others who have helped along the way include J. & D. Papworth, butchers and graziers with shops in Fakenham, Swaffham and Sheringham. We also had a real stroke of luck in the North of England when, having an hour to spare, we rang Stephen and Alison Morrell of Teesdale Game at Barnard Castle on the off chance that they might be able to help with providing a 'filler' photo of pigeons in the feather – they could and they did, but not only that, they were kind enough to offer us a copy of their recipe book, written in collaboration with professional author Malcolm L. Pearce. The book was part of Malcolm's 'The Easy Cook' series and entitled *The Game and Cheese Book*. In it were some superb ideas and recipes and so we subsequently wrote to Alison, Stephen and Malcolm requesting permission to include some in *The Pigeon Cook*. Permission was kindly granted, for which thanks are unreservedly offered.

Talking of permission to use words previously quoted in other books, we would like to acknowledge that given by Emily Johnson, Rights Manager of the Orion Publishing Group, for permission to quote from Mary Henderson's *Paris Embassy Cookbook*, published by Weidenfeld & Nicolson, an imprint of The Orion Publishing Group, London. The recipe for Chickpeas with Spinach, Raisins and Pine Nuts is taken from Louise Pickford's *The Olive Oil Cookbook*, first published by Salamander in 1994. Salamander is an imprint of Anova Books, London.

Whilst every effort has been made to ensure that permission has been sought and acknowledgements given, should anyone reading this book feel that that is not the case, we can only offer our apologies and the promise that, if they will be kind enough to get in touch with us via the publishers, we will make suitable amends in future reprints.

Of course no book can ever see the light of day without having someone to publish it! We would therefore very much like to thank everyone at The Crowood Press, who have perhaps the most difficult job of all – that of actually selling our books! Thank you all.

Introduction

Pigeons have been used as a food source for a very long time. The Romans kept them, and the manor houses of the Middle Ages would almost always contain a pigeon cote of some description on their premises. The squabs of wild pigeons were also taken from the nest just before they were due to fly, and to make sure they didn't disappear before that time, it was often the job of young rural workers to scramble up to the nests and attach a light cord to the leg of each squab. The cord would then be gently woven through the twigs of the nest and either tied to a lower branch or to a piece of stick which acted as a 'stop'. The squabs were thus free to move about in the nest but could not fly away, and were, when the time was right, collected and killed for their meat. And then, of course, there are the traditional shooting methods whereby woodpigeons are decoyed over the autumn stubble fields, or shot in February as they fly into roost, and during a general countryside mooch with dog and gun.

The pigeon's popularity is not just due to availability, but more because of its versatility, as will be seen in the many and varied recipes within this book. It can be plucked and dressed in the same way as a chicken or gamebird, or it can simply have its breast removed, which is then flash fried and served with a sauce or interesting summer salad. Young pigeons are perfect for almost any cooking method, whilst older ones can be usefully incorporated into casseroles, stews and game pies, where they add welcome variety to the other meats contained within the pastry.

Pigeons are the mainstay of much European cooking; in France, for example, wild pigeons may well be made into *salmis de palombes*, a dish where the bird is part-roasted and the breasts then carved from the bone and a sauce created from the legs and carcass, together with a whole host of other ingredients that might include wine, garlic, juniper berries and herbs – all of which are vital components of several recipes to be found in the 'Perfect Pigeon Recipes' chapter, thus acknowledging the importance of the French influence in much of what today's forward-thinking chefs like to cook. The Moroccans and Spanish include in their menus *bestilla* (sometimes spelt '*bistalia*'), a type of pigeon pie made with a sort of filo pastry, whilst in Italy there is the *casseruola del cacciatore*, quite literally a hunter's casserole containing halved woodpigeons, jointed rabbit, vegetables and wild mushrooms. In Egypt, according to Clarissa Dickson Wright, they rear domesticated pigeons and stuff them with green wheat or *farik*. So, as can be seen, the culinary interest in pigeon is not by any means confined to British shores, nor necessarily to simple fare – in fact in south-west France the *pigeon de Lauragais* is served in only the best restaurants and is sought out by the most discerning gastronomes who are happy to pay high prices for the privilege of doing so.

Pigeon topped with bacon makes a good combination.

At the other end of the scale, have you tried cooking pigeon kebab-style over a barbecue? If not, why not? There's no reason not to after looking at the recipe on page 47! Woodpigeons live on the best food around (as many farmers know to their cost!), and pigeon, both wild and domesticated, automatically lends itself to being accompanied by hedgerow fruits and berries that can be harvested during an autumnal walk, or to salad stuffs in the summer and vegetables straight from the garden in the autumn. Its meat is not 'gamey' to taste, a factor that may put off some from trying a well hung pheasant or grouse, and is instead perfect for almost any combination you may care to try. Even their eggs make for the basis of an interesting dish or two, and although they are not, it must be admitted, easy to come by, we have nevertheless included a couple of recipes for them.

Finally we make no apologies for including four or five recipes that first appeared in our book *Cook Game* (The Crowood Press, 2008): they are far too good not to pass on to new readers, and if you were kind enough to have bought a copy of *Cook Game* already, then worry not because contained within these pages there are many more completely new recipes for you to try!

Getting Started

How things change! Locally sourced produce was all that rural dwellers could hope for generations ago and, as such, much was made of rabbit, domesticated pigeon and woodpigeon from wherever and whenever they could be had. Then in the 1980s it was all nouvelle cuisine – small portions of anything fancy and ornate. Who would have believed, back then, that there was a fear that the character of food would change; that an ever-increasing use of fertilizers and chemicals would make vegetables taste bland and be of far less value nutritionally, and that the working population would end up eating only fast food and visiting take-away premises in preference to cosy restaurants where good food was lovingly prepared. Did any of that happen? Well, yes it did, but now, in the second decade of the twenty-first century, it seems that everything has come full circle, and whilst the occasional take-away continues to be a treat for some, far more are heading to gastro-pubs where good, locally sourced food can be had in pleasant, leisurely surroundings – and what frequently features on the menus and 'today's specials' boards but the ever-popular pigeon! Whilst we wouldn't want to tempt readers from enjoying such delights, we do however feel that with a little guidance, equally interesting culinary treats can be made in the kitchen of almost any and every household.

It is our firm belief that anyone can cook – however, to cook well and interestingly requires a little imagination and an ability to identify what goes with what. In addition, the way a dish is presented goes a long way towards the way in which it is received by the person to whom it is being offered. A white or pale-coloured plate on which is served a bland concoction of unprepossessing meat, rice and washed-out cabbage is not likely to tickle the taste buds, whereas the same plate, coloured with a rich red wine-infused sauce-covered pigeon breast accompanied by vibrant, in-season vegetables will surely have your guests salivating and eager to try the first mouthful.

But long before that there is the small matter of where one sources what is obviously the main ingredient – the pigeons themselves! During the game season when there is much general shooting done, it is possible to pick up woodpigeon from almost anywhere, but they are perhaps not quite as easy to find in the spring and summer unless you know the whereabouts of a local game dealer or someone regularly involved in helping a farmer to be clear of the type of crop damage so often associated with woodpigeon.

FIRST CATCH YOUR PIGEON!

Assuming that we are talking about woodpigeon here, the best way of ensuring the freshest birds is to go out and shoot them yourself! Pigeon shooting is a very popular sport which, at the time of writing, can be done all the year round – although currently some pressure has been brought to bear by certain lobbyists who wish to see woodpigeon being given a 'close' season in much the same way as game birds. Some shooting enthusiasts do, however, impose a voluntary close season on themselves and call a truce during the generally accepted breeding months from April to July (although, of course, pigeon will breed later into the year than this). Others argue that as an agricultural pest they should be shot throughout the year.

Roost Shooting

Normally an occupation of the winter months, roost shooting is, put simply, merely a question of identifying favoured roosting woods and tucking yourself out of sight in readiness for dusk and the arrival of any pigeons anxious to settle in the trees for the night. A few hours spent in reconnaissance are never wasted, and it will not be long before you are able to work out the birds' likely flight patterns. Where large numbers congregate, it should also be possible to find evidence of their presence by inspecting the forest floor and lower tree branches for faeces. In cold weather pigeons generally prefer warm woods containing firs, evergreens and ivy-clad trees situated in the lee of the prevailing wind or in a valley bottom over which the wind passes rather than whistling straight through.

Although roost shooting is popular throughout the winter months, it may be difficult to obtain permission to shoot on sporting estates until the pheasant shooting ends on 1 February. Understandably, land owners and gamekeepers will not want to risk disturbance to their carefully – and expensively – reared game birds at a time when shooting is in full swing. Come February, however, and permission may be more readily granted – especially if you already have 'a foot in the door' by having helped out on the shoot as a beater or picker-up during the pheasant-shooting season. In fact many shoots traditionally hold roost-shooting evenings on the first couple of Saturdays in February when the more shooters they have the merrier, as the main objective is to 'man' every wood with guns in order to keep birds on the move.

Shooting over Decoys

Decoy pigeons are many and varied. Realistic and lightweight decoys are available from most gunshops and agricultural suppliers, and on many of the stands at country shows. They may be simple half-shells that to a passing pigeon flying above, look like a feeding bird; a full-bodied version designed to be set on a stick to keep it above the height of the growing crop; or if you really want to get fancy, an all-singing, all-dancing affair set on an 'arm' which is activated by a battery. Purists often swear by a freshly shot pigeon carefully laid out in a realistic pose as being the best decoy, but to do that you have to first shoot your pigeon!

Whatever type is used, the whole point is to create a pattern of feeding pigeons set out on a piece of land where wild birds are known to want to fill their crops. Depending on the time of year, this may be when cereals are just emerging, young and tender, or when the harvest is completed and there is still any amount of wasted grain lying amongst the stubble. Whenever it may be, there is a great skill to decoying, which involves setting up your decoys in a random pattern acceptable to passing pigeons, and a carefully constructed hide from which you can shoot without being seen. Camouflage is of the essence here, as a woodpigeon's eyesight is notoriously excellent and can detect the whitey-pink of a forehead or the sunlit flash of a wrist watch. Be successful with your decoying, though, and you can be guaranteed some good, fleshy birds to take into the kitchen.

Pottering

It may be that any pigeons that come into the kitchen are gained as a result of 'pottering' with the gun on the rough shoot. They might not be your intended quarry, but whilst out on the off-chance of a rabbit or pheasant, if a pigeon or two clatters from the hedgerow and you are fortunate enough to be able to add them to the bag, they will make either a meal on their own or, when added to the other things shot that day, a very acceptable game pie or mixed game casserole – especially if, as a result of your pottering, you've been able to pick a fresh swede from the farmer's field or a handful of wild mushrooms, all of which can be added to the pot.

In the autumn, when birds have been feeding on acorns or sweet chestnuts, their crops will be quite literally full to bursting, and due to the abundance of this type of food, their meat is particularly flavoursome and 'nutty' to taste. In addition they will have a small layer of fat, which is a great help in cooking.

In particularly cold weather when the ground is frozen or snowed over, pigeons will flock heavily on to whatever available food is accessible. At this time of year it is likely

A dog, gun and a good 'eye' will almost always ensure that a few pigeons are in the bag at the end of the day.

to be kale or other crops grown specifically for livestock fodder, and it is not unusual to see the fields literally grey with birds anxious to fill their crops. In their desperation to feed they may be very easy to shoot, but whether they are worth bothering with is quite another matter due to the fact that, in such conditions, pigeons rapidly lose bodyweight and will make a very poor meal indeed.

Game Dealers, Butchers, Farmers' Markets and Elsewhere

If you are not in a position to acquire your own birds, then all is not lost as it is a simple matter to purchase them from your local game dealer (find him in *Yellow Pages*), a good old-fashioned butcher (a rare commodity, but hopefully still in your particular High Street) or at one of the increasingly popular farmers' markets, often held monthly at your nearest historical market town (your local library or tourist office should be able to help). Game, including pigeons, is also to be found for sale via the internet, and a quick trawl through a search engine will undoubtedly find someone who suits and is able to post your birds direct.

Your local shoot is another obvious alternative. If you make the effort to make yourself known and get involved with the shooting days as a beater, you will soon notice from the cheers down the line that many of the Guns take far greater delight in bringing down

A good traditional butcher's shop will quite often sell woodpigeons at certain times of the year, and will also be able to source reared table pigeons upon request.

a passing pigeon than they do in killing the highest, most difficult pheasant! If, during the course of the day, they also happen to shoot a woodcock or snipe, they will often ask to take that bird home – but not so the humble pigeon. As a result, you may find a spare pigeon or two left in the larder, and although the game dealer will happily take them when he comes to collect the day's bag, the estate gamekeeper is normally just as happy to let them go to those who have helped him on the day. It is also useful to have more than a passing acquaintance with a Gun on the local shoot, and if you make known your desire to try a particular pigeon dish, in all likelihood they will be able to supply you with what you need.

SKINNING, PLUCKING AND DRAWING

Skinning: Many of our pigeon recipes involve the use of the breast only. To remove the breast almost without having to pluck the bird, simply place it backside down on to a firm surface, then gently pull back and pluck the breast feathers until the keel (breast) bone can be seen, and with a sharp knife, cut through either side of the flesh as deep as possible until you have two liver-shaped pieces of meat. Then remove the skin (which is as easy as opening an envelope), and you should have the best of the bird ready and waiting to be incorporated into whatever recipe you are intending to use.

Plucking: If you require the whole carcass for a particular recipe then it will obviously be necessary to pluck the complete bird. Thankfully pigeons are one of the easiest, if not *the* easiest birds to pluck, and unlike game birds, their skin is not likely to rip during the process. Basically, either sit with the bird backside down between your knees, or put it on a firm surface with its head away from you, and begin to pluck the breast feathers backwards (against the direction of growth). You will soon learn the method, which can then be continued down the legs, along the back and up the neck. As there is very little meat on the wings of a pigeon, plucking these is a waste of time and it is far better to cut them off just before the 'shoulder' joint. Cut off the legs and feet exactly where the scaly part and the thigh meet (where the feathers stop). You will find a small, rounded bone joint which, if you cut round it and then twist the leg correctly, will break easily; as you pull the leg, it will bring the thigh muscle attachments with it.

Drawing: Cut off the head, insert a knife down the back of the neck, and open the skin. Chop off the neck bone near the body, and remove the gullet and the windpipe (you could add the neck to a stockpot, but the windpipe is of no use at all). The crop is joined to the gullet and is the thin bag at the end of the throat (depending on what the bird has been eating it could be gorged with greenstuffs, acorns, chestnuts or even ivy leaves). It may be freed by blunt dissection with the fingers, then severed from the rest of the gullet where it passes into the body cavity. Going to the other end of the bird, make a slit below the vent (in fact above it, because you will have the bird positioned uppermost). We always enlarge the slit by snipping right round the vent with scissors and freeing it entirely. Put one finger inside and free the viscera from the cavity walls by blunt dissection; when they feel totally free, gently pull out all the guts – first the gizzard, then the liver, and finally the heart and anything else left remaining. Unlike most birds, in pigeons there is no gall bladder attached to the liver (and therefore no need to take

Pigeon breasts are easy to remove from the carcass and prepare for cooking.

care that this small green sac is removed without splitting it, and so running the risk of contaminating the carcass).

STORING AND FREEZING

Unlike game birds, pigeons do not need hanging in order to get the best of their flavour: for the optimum taste pluck, draw and cook them as soon as possible after acquiring them. Sometimes you might not have a need for them immediately, or you might not have enough to make whatever recipe you have in mind – in which case it is important to have an organized freezer where everything is instantly accessible. An untidy heap of badly labelled and poorly stored birds can result in those at the very bottom never getting used and eventually being thrown away due to becoming 'out of date' or succumbing to the effects of freezer burn. Pigeons kept too long, whilst remaining usable, certainly tend to lose some of their flavour, and none should be kept frozen for more than twelve months at the very outside. Always keep a record of what goes in and what comes out, preferably on a wipe-clean board fixed close to where the freezer is kept.

A chest freezer is often best, provided that it contains sufficient trays to accommodate all of a specific game species; it is then a simple matter to lift out the other trays until

Although game dealers will chill down birds whilst in the feather, it is not good practice to do the same when home freezing, and pigeons should be plucked, drawn and sealed in freezer bags from which all surplus air has been expelled.

one has access to the particular one being sought. Within each tray, try and ensure that the oldest labelled bags are placed to the top so that their contents are always the first to be used, and ensure that any sharp or protruding wing or leg bones do not puncture the bag in which they are wrapped by wrapping them in kitchen foil. It is also important to make sure that all air is excluded from the bag by the simple expedient of inserting a drinking straw into the almost closed neck of the polythene bag and sucking it out.

STOREROOM INGREDIENTS

Many, in fact probably most of the recipes in this book do not require much that is not normally at hand in the kitchen of every enthusiastic chef. As a general practice, it always pays to use the best possible basic ingredients you can afford and to use them suitably. There are also a few standard ingredients that should be in the cupboards and store-room of every pigeon cook. Take care in storing them, though, and try to ensure that you follow the FIFO principles of commercial retailers – 'FIFO' standing for 'first in, first out': in that way you'll be sure of utilizing everything well before its 'best by' date.

- **Flour:** Useful for making pies and casserole lids, as well as for dusting pigeon breasts prior to frying – keep it in the larder, or, still in its bag, in a container made specifically for the purpose. Never mix old and new together when storing, and always use up one batch before you open the next.
- **Vegetable oil:** Reaches a higher heat in the frying pan than does olive oil, which is why it is used in deep-fat fryers. Personally, we prefer to use good quality virgin olive oil for virtually everything, but others have, alongside their standard bottle of olive oil, one containing perhaps a groundnut oil for frying and stir-frying, and the beautifully flavoured walnut and hazelnut oils for salad dressings – whatever you choose to do, always buy the best you can and store it in a dark place away from the heat of the hob.
- **Mustard:** A tin of good old-fashioned Colman's mustard powder is a good stand-by in any kitchen. Grainy French mustards are great added to casseroles or pot-roasts, and can, of course, be spooned straight from the pot and to the side of the plate in order to add 'zest' to a huge variety of pigeon dishes.
- **Salt and pepper:** During cooking, the addition of both salt and pepper is, in most cases, warranted. Every chef to whom we've spoken mentioned Maldon sea salt as their first priority, closely followed by table and cooking salt. As for pepper, it seems there is only one kind as far as most are concerned, and that is the aromatic black peppercorn (which is technically a spice). Keep the peppercorns whole and grind them as needed by the use of a wooden peppermill.
- **Herbs:** Although there can be nothing better than freshly chopped herbs that will give a special flavour not found in the dried varieties, there is still very much a case to be argued for the use of commercially dried herbs; however, it is important not to be too heavy-handed in their use because the initial drying of them seems to concentrate their flavour potential, and they could overpower the taste of some of the more subtle pigeon dishes. Ideally one should grow one's own herbs in the garden or on the kitchen windowsill, drying them in summer for later use. Most fresh herbs freeze very well, however, keeping their green colour and much more aroma and flavour than those that have been dried.
- **Garlic:** Will keep for about two weeks after being peeled and chopped, provided it is kept in oil in the refrigerator. Reference is also made to 'Lazy Garlic' in various recipes: this is the cheat's answer to all that tedious peeling, scraping and chopping – it can be bought in jars from the supermarkets, and all that is needed is for a teaspoon or so to be used in place of garlic cloves.
- **Spices:** Should be bought in small quantities because they do not retain their flavour for long. Just as black pepper has a more subtle flavour when freshly ground, so most other spices not only taste stronger, but very different when freshly ground or grated. A small hand-turned coffee grinder is ideal for most spices.
- **Pre-prepared sauces:** A bottle of tomato ketchup would perhaps be considered an insult to the chef if it were to be actually used on a prepared dish when brought to the table, but it has many uses during the preparation of some recipes. For example, when minced pigeon breast is used for nothing more elaborate than an ingredient of shepherd's pie, it can benefit from being flavoured by a good squirt or two of tomato ketchup. Try also mushroom ketchup as an alternative in the same sort of dishes. Lea

& Perrin's Worcestershire Sauce gives, according to the makers, 'that instant richness to meat dishes'. It is also a very valuable ingredient in the creating of marinades. Soy and oyster sauces also have their followers.

COOKING UTENSILS

Whatever you have in the kitchen should suffice, but a heavy-bottomed casserole dish that can withstand heat from the hob as well as heat from the oven, together with a 'proper' cast-iron frying pan, are both essential for the pigeon cook. Two or three differently sized saucepans will be needed – look to buy those made of heavy stainless steel or anodized aluminium, both materials that allow for even heat distribution. Copper pans are excellent, if somewhat expensive; depending on how much cooking you are intending to do, they may well require 'relining' from time to time. Having said that, always buy the best you can afford otherwise you will be forever screwing back handles that have become loose or, worse still, constantly buying new ones.

Kitchen knives are one thing you should not stint on and, once again, buy the best you can reasonably afford – not normally impressed by brand names, we do however, on this occasion, think that a knife made by a well-known manufacturer is a 'must'. Good, very sharp knives save both time and patience. The size and type are largely a matter of personal choice, but it is a good idea to keep a special one for vegetable peeling and one for cutting up meat. If you have a dual-purpose knife for these, it has to be constantly washed between operations.

As long as you keep them dry, clean and sharp, your knives will serve you for many years to come. When we were at The Bell at Horndon on the Hill, Essex, chefs Stuart Fry and Stephen Treadwell told us of knives made from zirconium carbide: apparently they should not need sharpening for at least five years (after which time, you will, it must be admitted, have to send them away to be sharpened rather than be able to do it yourself). We were much taken by the idea and are determined to buy one (they are not cheap, however – an internet 'trawl' suggests you might need to pay upwards of £50). On the down side, the way the handles are constructed apparently makes it uncomfortable to use one for several hours a day, but providing you are not a professional chef who would obviously need to do so, they sound as if they could be the perfect solution to the perennial problem of blunt knives.

A fair selection of wooden spoons of different shapes and sizes must be considered. Small ones with one flattened side are invaluable for sauces as they can get into the edges of the pan, whilst a perforated or slotted metal spoon is useful for removing pigeon breasts from sauces and casseroles as required. High heat rubber spatulas and whisks should find a place in your kitchen armoury, as must incidentals such as wooden skewers, a meat tenderizer, a garlic press, funnels, sieves and colanders. Don't forget a potato peeler, a masher and a can opener. A pestle and mortar can be useful when it comes to pounding down peppercorns and spices.

Cutting boards are also important: you'll probably require two – one for vegetables and for rolling out pastry for pie tops, the other for cutting and preparing raw meat. To avoid confusion, it is a good idea to have them in different colours, or at least mark them in some way. A selection of 'Pyrex'-type mixing bowls will be needed, and never underestimate the importance of Tupperware containers – the joy of these is that they are freezer, microwave and dishwasher safe, as well as being the perfect vessel in which to store unused fresh herbs.

As far as mechanical aids are concerned, a food processor is undoubtedly a useful piece of kit – but great results can still be obtained without one, they will simply take longer to achieve! A hand-held blender can be used for many different purposes, especially when making sauces and soups. Whilst we hardly ever use them (much preferring to work by 'eye'), kitchen scales are nevertheless crucial on occasions, as are a couple of liquid measuring jugs.

CLEANLINESS IN THE KITCHEN

Consider this extract taken from Mary Henderson's *Paris Embassy Cookbook*, published in 1980 by Weidenfeld and Nicolson:

> The chef, Monsieur James Viaëne, is of Flemish origin; his grandfather was Belgian. He is unflappable and a master of organization. Whether he is preparing a dinner for fifty or a buffet for two hundred and fifty, the kitchens remain spotless: the copper pans glisten, the pastry boards are dusted with flour as if touched by a light frost; balloon whisks, sieves, strainers and spatulas are used, washed and put back in place with clockwork precision. An atmosphere of concentration and creation reigns.

Although it is unlikely that you will ever be in the position of having to cater for 250 guests (or even fifty, for that matter), the way that M. Viaëne obviously ran his kitchen is one to be emulated. Surfaces on which food is to be prepared should be cleaned daily, and certainly before you begin. Match your cleaning product to your surface type, but steer clear of any abrasives because they will shorten the lifespan of the surfaces: in fact, consider using items that you will already have as cooking ingredients as cleaning ingredients. Baking soda, for instance, is suitable for removing most common household stains from surfaces: use two or three tablespoons of baking soda per cup of warm water and gently remove grease and stubborn splatters with a sponge. Afterwards, rinse down with cold water and dab with a paper kitchen towel.

Cooking of any description can be a messy affair and it will not be long before something gets spilt. The natural reaction is obviously to wipe it up straightaway, but if you do so with less-than-clean cloths and sponges, there is always the risk that you will be contaminating rather than cleaning. Recent research by the Royal London Hospital noted that many domestic kitchen cloths and sponges tested were harbouring bacteria that could be responsible for *E. coli* and salmonella infections.

Keep your cloths and sponges clean by washing them in hot, soapy water and then placing them in a suitable disinfectant before rinsing and allowing them to dry thoroughly. There is apparently nothing to be gained in soaking them overnight, as disinfectant solutions weaken over a period of time. Alternatively, heat them for one minute in a microwave, or place them in a dishwasher operating with a drying cycle. Sponges that were put through either a dishwasher or a microwave were found to hold less than 1 per cent of moulds and yeasts, whereas those soaked in a chlorine bleach solution allowed a frighteningly higher percentage to survive. It makes you think, doesn't it?

A FEW RANDOM THOUGHTS

At risk of being accused of teaching grandmother to suck eggs – or indeed cook pigeon – it might still be worth mentioning a few basic points concerning general preparation in the kitchen.

- A garden shed, outhouse or utility room is by far the best place to prepare one's pigeon. Even if it is a simple matter of just cutting out the breasts and therefore there is no actual plucking to be done, we can guarantee that you'll be finding the occasional pigeon feather for days afterwards – and if you don't, your cat will! If there really is no alternative and you need to pluck a bird, do so into the confines of a plastic bin bag that will at least catch the majority of feathers.
- Wipe, rather than wash pigeon breasts, and do not prepare them on sheets of newspaper – use a chopping board instead.
- Wipe your chopping board straightaway afterwards, indeed make it a personal mantra to clear up as you go – most modern houses have tiny kitchens that never have enough work surfaces, and if you are a messy cook, you will undoubtedly end up with no space, peeled onion skins floating around, carrot tops on the floor where they fell as you chopped them, and sauce rings wherever you laid down your wooden spoon after stirring.
- Read every recipe first and make sure you have all the ingredients – although a last minute substitution on the discovery that you've only got shallots rather than onions will probably not affect the success of a particular recipe, the absence of juniper berries for a sauce in which they are the major ingredient is perhaps not so easy to overcome.
- Having said that, never be frightened of experimenting with less vital ingredients, and just because a certain recipe suggests that 'x' should be used, don't for one minute think that the recipe will not be equally as successful with 'y'. Necessity is, as they say, the Mother of invention – but imagination is the Father of success.
- Cooking of any description should be systematic and well thought out. In an ideal world you should be able to work on a surface immediately to either left or right of your oven and hob top: reach to your left for the vegetable rack, the right for access to your pots and pans, and above for the shelves and cupboards that contain all the possible incidental 'bits and pieces'.
- There is an expression that goes along the lines of 'keep your friends close, and your enemies ever closer': keep your knives and other tools of the trade close to hand, and they will never have the chance to become your enemies!

The pigeon as an art form! Part of a painting on the wall of the restaurant at The Old Bridge, Huntingdon.

Perfect Pigeon Recipes

Describing her husband's ability to construct a meal out of nothing, a lady of our acquaintance recently commented:

> He just plunders the store cupboard (and drinks cupboard), sees what there is and concocts a recipe round it. He'll always find a way to use up off bits of bacon and cheese in the fridge and a few less-than-fresh-looking vegetables at the back of the rack; ask him to reproduce the same recipe for a second time and he cannot – not because he can't remember, but more because the ingredients around him change from week to week as a result of what's been bought from the butchers, shot on the local shoot or dug up out of the garden. At the end of the shooting season he'll dive into the freezer and bring out whatever odd bits of meat are left in there and make the hugest game pie which we then have cold and end up living off for days afterwards.

Now, apart from possibly making the most of us lesser mortals who make up the majority of the male population feel inadequate, our friend's observations on her husband's cooking style illustrate very well the fact that cooking with pigeon (or virtually any other main ingredient for that matter) is merely a question of using one's imagination. Remember, therefore, that many of the recipes included in the following pages need not be followed slavishly, and that many can be adapted, experimented with, or simply read through in order to gain a few ideas.

Unless otherwise stated, the recipes are sufficient for four people. However, such is the nature of many pigeon dishes (especially those that are salad based) that by adjusting the quantities they can be substantial main meals, appetizers and starters, or tasty lunch dishes. It is, therefore, impracticable to subdivide the chapter into 'starters' and 'mains', and it is up to the reader to decide what recipe is best fitted to what purpose.

MARINADES

Sometimes a recipe calls for pigeon breasts to be marinated. Marinades help to break down meat fibres as well as imbibing them with subtle tastes. They also counteract the possibility of dryness as the meat cooks. There is no exact science to preparing a marinade, but a typical one may well combine some or all of the following ingredients:

A bottle of red wine
2 tablespoons of red wine vinegar
  (or rather less of balsamic)
Chopped onion and garlic
Herbs

A pinch of mixed dried spices and
  the same of grated nutmeg
A bay leaf or two
A couple of 'glugs' of olive oil
Half-a-dozen juniper berries,
  if you can get them

You may prefer to omit all but the slightest amount of wine, replacing it with rather more olive oil.

As an interesting alternative, make a Chinese-style marinade by bringing together the following:

1 finely chopped onion
2 crushed cloves of garlic

1 tablespoon of freshly grated ginger
2 teaspoons of chopped parsley

Add liquid consisting of:

¼ cup of lemon juice
¼ cup of sesame oil

2 tablespoons of soy sauce
2 tablespoons of honey

Not only will this make an excellent marinade, but the mixture can also be brushed over meat when grilling or barbecuing.

Marinade ingredients typically required for many pigeon dishes.

Pigeon Pie

The internet is very useful in so many ways. You cannot possibly have a book containing pigeon recipes without including one for pigeon pie. Surprisingly, none of the pubs and restaurants we contacted offered one and so we resorted to the World Wide Web – and what a plethora of choice there is! Finally we selected this one from Gourmet Britain, and on contacting Simon Scrutton for permission, he was only too pleased to allow us to use it. Gourmet Britain really is the perfect site for all of us who are interested in food: it offers a huge database of all things gourmet, suppliers of local produce, mail-order opportunities, good restaurants, recipes and places to stay. As Heston Blumenthal wrote in the *Sunday Times*: 'Gourmet Britain [is] a fantastic resource of artisan producers and mail-order suppliers around the country, both for meat and other elusive ingredients.' Can there ever be a better testimonial?

4 pigeons (ask your butcher to remove
the breasts, but to give you the carcasses
for use as stock)
30g/1oz butter
1 medium onion, peeled and sliced
1 large carrot, peeled and cut into very
small dice
1 medium clove of garlic, peeled and finely
chopped
6 thin slices of streaky bacon
½ teaspoon paprika

A little salt and a few grinds of freshly milled
black peppercorns
½ teaspoon *herbes de Provence*
2 tablespoons freshly chopped parsley
6 medium potatoes, peeled and thinly sliced
4 hard-boiled eggs, cut into quarters
225g/8oz puff pastry (a frozen packet will
take the effort out of making your own,
but try to find an all-butter variety)
1 egg, lightly beaten

For the stock

The carcasses of the pigeons (the legs
and thighs can be removed and frozen
for another occasion, if you feel you will
use them)
1 medium onion, peeled and roughly chopped
1 clove of garlic, peeled

1 medium carrot, peeled and roughly
chopped
1 stick of celery
1 bay leaf
1 glass of red wine
6 black peppercorns

Put all the stock ingredients into a saucepan and add about 850ml/1½ pints of water, or more if you need more to cover the solid items. Bring this to the boil, reduce the heat so you maintain a bare simmer, then cook for 30 minutes: remove any scum if it appears.

Remove from the heat, strain, discard the solids and set the stock to one side.

Cut each pigeon breast into three pieces, across their length (giving you chunky, rather than long pieces).

Melt the butter over a low heat, add the chopped onions, and sweat them until they are translucent, but not brown. Add the bacon, garlic and carrots, and fry for a further 2 minutes.

Remove from the heat; add the salt, paprika, pepper, pigeon breast pieces, *herbes de Provence* and parsley. Mix this all together and put a thin layer of the meat mixture in the base of your chosen pie dish; cover with a layer of potatoes, then add a few of the hard-boiled egg quarters, repeating this until you have used all the solid ingredients. Add enough stock to cover the meat and potatoes, but no more.

If you are intending to bake the pie straightaway, heat the oven to gas mark 4/180°C.

On a cold worktop, roll out the pastry fairly thinly, using a little flour to stop it sticking – aim for a shape rather larger than the pie dish. Then cut some thin lengths of pastry (about 2.5cm/1in wide), and paint these with a little of the beaten egg. Stick these, egg-washed-side down, around the perimeter of the pie dish; then paint them with a little more egg wash on their top surface.

Cover the pie with the pastry, and trim off any excess. Make a few holes in the 'lid' to allow any steam to escape. Brush the top of the pastry with the remaining egg wash, ensuring you don't block up the escape holes.

Bake the pie in the preheated oven for 1 hour, lowering the heat to gas mark 3/160°C after half an hour.

Remove from the oven, and rest at room temperature for 5 minutes before serving.

Smothered Pigeons

How this basic casserole came by the name it has, we've no idea, but it originates from North America where the foundation of their kitchen is, we believe, predominantly British. Having said that, there is, in Germany, a recipe for *Geschmorte Schweinerippin*, which translates as 'smothered pork chops', so perhaps the name is, in fact, European in origin.

4 small pigeons	1 sliced carrot
115g/4oz plain flour	2 celery sticks, sliced
115g/4oz butter	300ml/10fl oz game or chicken stock
Salt and pepper	Parsley, for garnish
1 chopped onion	

Dredge the pigeons in flour seasoned with salt and pepper.

Melt the butter in a heavy-bottomed, hob-proof casserole dish, and brown the pigeons on both sides without burning the butter (which would impart a bitter taste). Add the vegetables, stir them about well, and pour in the stock. Cover and place in the oven at gas mark 5/190°C for about an hour.

Season again (if necessary) prior to serving, and garnish with fresh chopped parsley.

Roast Breast of Holkham Pigeon, Toasted Brioche, Rhubarb and Redcurrant Compote with Black Peppercorn Ice Cream

If you ever have cause to be in the Downham Market area of Norfolk, make a point of nipping into The Hoste Arms, even if it is just for afternoon tea or a drink. Better still, try and arrange an overnight stay there. It is owned by Paul Whittome, co-founder of the hugely successful 'Great Inns of Britain' organization, and as such you can be sure of the freshest linen, the finest local produce and the friendliest staff. Andrew McPherson joined The Hoste Arms in 1991 as their executive chef and is now a director. He and his staff made us very welcome whilst we were on our travels in search of recipes for this book. Particular thanks must be given to Gemma Arnold, who came in on her day off to prepare the recipes so that we could photograph them.

Pan-fry two pigeons in butter until golden all round, and then roast for 8–10 minutes at gas mark 6/200°C before 'resting' for 10 minutes.

Remove the breasts and set aside in a warm place.

Roast Breast of Holkham Pigeon, Toasted Brioche, Rhubarb and Redcurrant Compote with Black Peppercorn Ice Cream.

For the rhubarb and redcurrant compote

150g/5½oz sugar
1ltr/1¾ pint water

300g/10½oz rhubarb, chopped
30g/1oz redcurrants

Boil the sugar and water, and add the rhubarb. Simmer over a low heat until the rhubarb is softening, add the redcurrants, and continue cooking until the rhubarb is soft.

For the brioche

3 eggs
30ml/1fl oz warmed milk
15g/½oz sugar
250g/9oz flour

175g/6oz softened butter
Pinch of salt
1 egg yolk

Gently combine the eggs, milk, sugar and flour. Add the butter and salt, and beat together well.

Line two loaf tins with a little butter, and dust with flour. Place the brioche dough into the tins, brush egg yolk over the top, and leave to 'prove'.

Place in an oven at gas mark 4/180°C for 25 minutes. If the bottom sounds hollow when tapped, the loaves are ready.

Leave on a rack to cool.

For the black peppercorn ice cream

250ml/8fl oz cream

250ml/8fl oz milk

100g/3½oz crushed black peppercorns

225g/8oz egg yolks

225g/8oz caster sugar

Bring the cream, milk and crushed peppercorns to the boil. Whisk the egg yolks and sugar in a separate bowl, then add the cream/milk mixture to the eggs/sugar, mixing well.

Return the mixture to the saucepan, and place on a low heat in order to cook out the egg. Using a wooden spoon, stir gently and continuously. The *anglaise* is ready when a clear line is visible on the back of the spoon (be careful not to scramble the eggs, says Gemma).

Cool until set, and assemble the dish as shown in the photograph.

The Hoste Arms.

Pigeon in Pears

Not quite a partridge in a pear tree, but a good recipe nevertheless! Depending on appetites around the table you might wish to cook the pigeons and then remove the breasts before serving, rather than present a whole bird to each diner.

4 woodpigeons, skinned
30g/1oz butter
1 tablespoon redcurrant jelly
150ml/5fl oz chicken stock

150ml/5fl oz heavy red wine
Salt and freshly ground black pepper
4 small dessert pears, peeled and quartered

Brown the pigeons by placing them with the butter in a large hob-proof casserole dish. Stir in the redcurrant jelly, stock, wine and seasoning to taste.

Bring to the boil, then reduce the heat before adding the pears. Cover the dish and simmer gently for approximately three-quarters of an hour.

Remove the pigeons and pears from the dish, and keep warm.

For the beurre manié
2 tablespoons butter
1 tablespoon plain flour

4 tablespoons double cream
1 bunch of watercress for garnish

Mix the two tablespoons of butter with the tablespoon of flour and add, in small pieces, to the cooking liquid, stirring continuously. The sauce should thicken quite quickly.

Then very slowly and carefully, incorporate the cream whilst heating gently (but do not allow the liquid to boil otherwise the mixture will curdle).

Pour some of the sauce over the pigeons and serve the rest in a jug. Use the watercress to garnish.

Pigeon Hot-Pot Sausages and Pears

The next time you are at the butcher's buying meat, pick your moment to catch him in a good mood and ask him nicely for a few natural sausage skins with which to try this recipe. You might also need to save up a few pigeons from your shooting expeditions in order to have sufficient breast meat to try it!

1.5kg/3½lb minced pigeon breast
3 carrots, peeled and finely chopped
1 large onion, peeled and finely chopped
3 'Maris Piper' potatoes, peeled and chopped
Oil or butter to sauté

Salt and pepper
Quantity of natural sausage skins
Oil for frying
2–3 large dessert pears, peeled, cored and
    sliced

For the (optional) rosemary gravy
Glug of red wine   500ml/18fl oz stock
Pinch of rosemary

Sauté the onion, potatoes and carrots in a heavy-bottomed pan containing oil or butter. Mix well with the minced pigeon, and season.

If you have no sausage machine, stuff the mixture into the sausage skins by using a piping bag equipped with a large nozzle. Twist the ends and leave the sausages overnight (otherwise the skins will split when cooking).

Fry in oil for about two or three minutes, and then transfer the sausages to a roasting tin. Surround them with the pear slices, and in an oven pre-heated to gas mark 6/200°C, cook them for a further 5 to 10 minutes (the pear slices should 'caramelize' with the juices from the sausages and soften whilst doing so).

Serve with mashed potatoes and, if you like, some rosemary gravy made by pouring a good glug of red wine into a pan, adding a pinch of rosemary and reducing the liquid by half. Add roughly 500ml/18fl oz of cold water into which veal stock concentrate has been added. Heat until the gravy thickens. (You could use ordinary chicken or vegetable stock instead of the veal concentrate/cold water mix.)

Pigeon Breasts with Pineapple and Almonds

Not long into the millennium we went to Italy with the idea of doing some research for a book – the book unfortunately never saw the light of publication, but we did return home with a recipe idea as the result of staying at a very rural farmhouse where we were served goose breast with pineapple and almonds. Bearing in mind the fact that goose breasts obviously contain more fat than those of pigeons and can be pan-fried without additional fats, we suggest that compensation is made by frying them in butter. Also, the original recipe used a fresh pineapple, complete with its crown of leaves. The crown was removed prior to peeling the rest and cutting the flesh into segments, and the crown was then used as a focal point at the centre of the dish, around which the meal was brought to the table. However, unless you are really out to impress, tinned segments of pineapple will work just as well. Other than these few minor adjustments, the recipe here is pretty much as we remember it!

8 pigeon breasts
4 tablespoons flour
Knob of butter
Salt and freshly ground pepper
1 small glass brandy
1 cup pineapple juice (from the tin or bought as breakfast juice)

1 tablespoon white wine vinegar
1 small pineapple (or a large tin of unsweetened segments)
1 tablespoon blanched almonds, 'toasted' in a heated dry frying pan and roughly chopped

Dust the pigeon breasts in flour, and pan-fry them in the butter until browned but the juices are still running pink. Season, and pour over the brandy. Remove them from the pan and wrap in foil to keep warm (they will continue to cook slightly, hence the need for them to be slightly underdone when removed from the pan).

Add the pineapple juice and the wine vinegar to the juices in the pan; heat to thicken before adding the pineapple segments and a little more butter. Once the segments are warmed through, cut the pigeon breasts diagonally so as to form long, oblique slices, and serve on a plate with a little of the sauce and segments poured over. Top off with the chopped almonds; serve the remainder of the sauce in a jug.

As an idea, try serving this dish with Jersey New Potatoes with Onions and Olive Oil (see page 76).

Potted Smoked Pigeon with Duck Legs and Chicken Breast

We included a recipe for potted Goosnargh duck in our book *The New Country Cook* (The Crowood Press, 2009) and have adapted it here to include pigeon breasts. The original recipe was a result of our travels round the North West, and was suggested by Alice Booth, one of our bed-and-breakfast hosts.

Makes six ramekins

2 large duck legs	Small handful of fresh thyme
500g/1lb 2oz clarified butter	Salt and pepper
4 cloves garlic, crushed	Small handful fresh parsley, finely chopped

To smoke the duck and chicken breasts

1 level tablespoon rice	125g/4½oz pigeon breast
1 level tablespoon brown sugar	125g/4½oz chicken breast
1 level tablespoon tea leaves	1 lemon or lime, finely sliced

Place the duck legs, butter, garlic, thyme, salt and pepper into a roasting pot, cover and bake slowly for 2 hours at gas mark 2/150°C. At the end of cooking, the meat should just fall off the bone. When cooked, strip the meat and retain the butter mixture.

Line the bottom of a wok with tinfoil, making sure you leave enough foil up the sides to protect the sides of your wok. Place the rice, sugar and tea leaves on the foil, and then cut another piece of foil to loosely cover them. On this circle of foil, lay the pigeon and chicken breasts plus a few slices of lemon or lime.

If the wok has a lid, cover it now, otherwise use a third piece of foil and fix it so as to form a secure 'lid' through which no smoke can escape. Smoke for 10–15 minutes by placing the wok on a hob.

Remove the breasts and finish them off by cooking them in a hot oven for a further 5 minutes. Once cooked, finely chop them and add them, together with the shredded leg meat, to the clarified butter you have retained. Mix in the parsley and spoon the mixture into the ramekin dishes.

Potted Pigeon and Game, as served at The Rose and Crown, Romaldkirk, Co. Durham.

Place them in the fridge to set overnight.

Serve as a starter with warm toast.

Note: Make clarified butter by carefully melting unsalted butter over a low heat until three separate layers form. Skim off the top layer of froth. At the bottom of the pan will be a milky layer of sediment. The pure yellow liquid that is left is clarified butter. Remove the saucepan from the heat and allow to rest for a few minutes, then strain the clarified butter through a fine sieve or a cheesecloth-lined strainer.

Pigeon Breasts with Cassis and Raspberries

As well as juniper berries, which feature quite frequently in this collection of pigeon recipes, other berried fruits 'marry' extremely well with pigeon. Experiment by substituting blackberries or, as we've done here, raspberries.

8 pigeon breasts, with the skin still attached
Butter or oil (or a mixture of the two) for frying
2 teaspoons sea salt
2 teaspoons ground cinnamon
4 teaspoons Demerara sugar

A little black pepper
250ml/8fl oz red wine
150ml/5fl oz crème de cassis
1 tablespoon cornflour
225g/8oz fresh raspberries

In a frying pan heat the butter/oil and fry the pigeon breasts skin side down until the skin browns. Remove with a slotted spoon (if there is a surplus of fat, pour away most, but not all of it).

Place the salt, sugar and cinnamon in a bowl: mix and then sprinkle over the pigeon breasts, using your fingers to rub the mixture in well; then season with the pepper. Reheat the frying pan and cook the breasts skin side up for a further 5 to 8 minutes. Remove from the pan and allow to rest.

Pour the wine and cassis into a jug; use a little of the alcohol to mix with the cornflour, then return the resultant runny paste to the jug. The frying pan should still contain about two tablespoons of butter/oil/pigeon juices: place it back on the heat and add the alcohol/cornflour mix, and simmer for 2 or 3 minutes until this sauce has thickened. Add the raspberries and cook long enough just to warm the berries through.

Place the pigeon breasts under the grill for about a minute (in which time the sugar should begin to caramelize). Remove and slice the breasts; pour over a little of the sauce and serve immediately. The remainder of the sauce can be jugged and served at the table.

Roast Holkham Pigeon Breasts, Braised Puy Lentils, Lardons and Salsa Verde

This is another recipe from The Hoste Arms, Downham Market, Norfolk. The restaurant sources much of their game from the local butchers, who in turn collect it from the very well known Holkham estate in the centre of prime Norfolk shooting country. We were very well looked after, and Jeremy considers that he slept in the largest bed he'd ever seen, so huge he thought he might need a taxi to travel from one side of it to the other!

Pan-fry the pigeons in the butter until golden all round, and then roast for 8–10 minutes at gas mark 6/200°C; allow to 'rest' for 10 minutes. Remove the breasts and set aside in a warm place.

2 sticks celery	200g/7oz Puy lentils (soak overnight)
2 carrots	Stock
4 banana shallots	Lardons of pancetta
1 leek	Oil for frying

Finely dice all the vegetables and sauté briefly, add the Puy lentils and enough stock to cover, and simmer over a low heat until cooked. Season to taste. Julienne the lardons of pancetta and fry in a little oil, then use as shown in the accompanying photograph.

For the salsa verde

1 bunch of fresh basil	30g/1oz gherkins, finely chopped
¼ teaspoon of Dijon mustard	2 cloves garlic
30g/1oz capers, finely chopped	200ml/7fl oz olive oil

Roast Holkham Pigeon Breasts, Braised Puy Lentils, Lardons and Salsa Verde.

Whizz all the ingredients together in a food processor, and assemble the components of the dish as shown.

Pigeon Bruschetta

For the country person, the great thing about woodpigeons is that at certain times of the year they are easy to get hold of, and reasonably cheap should you have to pay for them. With this in mind, it is always worth developing your own ideas into tried and trusted recipes. This is the result of just such an experiment! It will serve four people as a starter, but only two for lunch.

30ml/1fl oz (a couple of tablespoons!) red wine vinegar
60ml/2fl oz olive oil (and a little more to drizzle over the bruschetta)
1 shallot, very thinly sliced
Salt and pepper

Oil for frying
8 pigeon breasts
4 slices of French bread or baguette cut on the diagonal
Garlic clove

Mix together the vinegar, oil and sliced shallot in a bowl. Season with the salt and pepper and marinate the pigeon breasts for a couple of hours.

Place a small amount of oil in a frying pan and heat until smoking. Season the pigeon breasts and cook in the hot oil for about 1 minute on each side. Allow to rest whilst the bruschetta toast is being cooked.

If you have a ridged griddle, heat it until it is very hot and toast the French bread slices on each side until they are golden brown (otherwise toast them under an ordinary grill); with a sharp knife, cut three indentations into each one and rub in the garlic clove, then drizzle over a little good quality olive oil.

Carve the pigeon breasts into slices, and lay the slices on the bruschetta. Garnish with watercress tossed in a few drops of French dressing.

Pigeon, Mushroom and Watercress Bap

Not really a sandwich to pack in foil and take out into the countryside for a day's sporting activity or on a long hike, as it needs to be eaten warm; it does, however, make a mouth-watering lunch-time snack for one person.

1–2 pigeon breasts, cut into strips of
   approximately 1cm/½in
Salt and pepper
2 teaspoons butter
A handful (before slicing) of mushrooms

A tight handful of watercress leaves
1 tablespoon mayonnaise
1 large day-old white bap, or a small plain
   teacake, cut in half lengthways

Season the pigeon strips, then sauté in one teaspoonful of the butter. Remove from the pan and set aside in a warming oven.

Add the second teaspoon of butter to the pan and fry the sliced mushrooms for about 2 minutes. Remove from the pan with a slotted spoon, and put to one side with the meat pieces.

Toast the bread bap, and whilst this is doing, very quickly wilt the watercress leaves in the juices left in the frying pan. Put the leaves into a bowl, stir in the mayonnaise, and spoon the mixture on to one side of the toasted bread bap or teacake.

Add the pigeon pieces together with the mushrooms, and close with the top half of the sandwich.

A few slices of fresh dessert pear could be added to the plate as an accompaniment, and a glass of local-brewed beer would most certainly add to this particular taste experience!

Pigeons Saint-Germain

Like the recipe for *Pigeons à la Française*, this recipe is a much copied classic.

55g/2oz slice of salt belly pork or green streaky
   bacon, diced
4 pigeons
12 pickling-sized onions (blanched)

1 tablespoon flour
200ml/7fl oz chicken stock, or canned
   consommé

1kg/2¼lb fresh green peas, shelled	Salt and pepper
3 juniper berries	200ml/7fl oz apple juice
Sprig of thyme	

Put the belly pork into a flameproof heavy casserole and place over a gentle heat in order to draw out the fat. Add the pigeons and onions to the pan; cook until brown on all sides, then remove from the pan. Blend in the flour and cook until browned. Pour in the stock and stir until smooth.

Replace the pigeons and onions, add the peas, juniper berries, thyme and seasoning. Cover and simmer gently for about 40 minutes.

Take out the pigeons, split in half and cut away the backbone and legs. Return the pigeon to the casserole, pour on the apple juice and reheat. At the end of cooking, the sauce should be of a creamy thickness, so add extra thickening if necessary.

Season to taste just before serving.

Breast of Holkham Pigeon with Vietnamese Coleslaw

This is yet another recipe from The Hoste Arms at Downham Market. Thanks again to all of you who looked after us so well!

Many pigeon recipes require the bird to be left to 'rest' before the breasts are taken off the bone.

For the coleslaw

1 red onion	80g/3oz sugar
¼ red cabbage	25ml/1fl oz liquid glucose
2 carrots	½ red chilli
100g/3½oz bean shoots	2 tablespoons sweet soy sauce
¼ bunch coriander	2 tablespoons rice wine vinegar
30g/1oz honey-roasted peanuts	1 teaspoon Thai fish sauce
Salt	4 pigeons

Finely shred the vegetables and mix together with the coriander, nuts and salt. Boil the sugar, glucose, chilli and soy sauce until you have a light syrup. Add the rice wine vinegar and fish sauce. Reboil, and pour over the vegetables, then place the coleslaw in the fridge for a few hours.

Seal the pigeons in a hot pan and then cook in the oven at gas mark 7/220°C for 8–10 minutes. Leave to rest for 5 minutes and take the breast off the bone. Simply serve the breasts warm on top of the coleslaw and dress with a little olive oil – it's a dish that doesn't need any fuss, as the flavours will speak for themselves.

Austrian Stuffed Pigeon

Thirty years or so ago, the Hotel Weisses Kreuz in Innsbruck used to serve a very similar dish to this classic Austrian recipe. The Weisses Kreuz dates back to 1465, when it began life as a small inn giving shelter to merchants and farmers. From memory, its old-style charm made a perfect backdrop to the dish – especially when it was preceded by a glass or two of Glühwein on a cold winter's day!

4 young pigeons	55g/2oz fine breadcrumbs, fried in a little butter
55g/2oz butter	Redcurrant jelly
150ml/5fl oz soured cream	

For the stuffing

115g/4oz calves' liver, chopped	1 dessertspoon chopped thyme
4 anchovy fillets, chopped	Salt and black pepper
4 juniper berries, chopped	55g/2oz butter
1 large onion, peeled and finely chopped	

Make the stuffing by frying all the ingredients in the butter until tender. Stuff the pigeons and roast them in butter, basting occasionally, at gas mark 6/200°C for 15–20 minutes, or until cooked. When ready for the table, pour a little of the soured cream over each of them and serve with the fried breadcrumbs accompanied by redcurrant jelly.

NB: For more stuffing alternatives, see Chapter 3.

GLÜHWEIN

Glühwein is mentioned in the Austrian Stuffed Pigeon recipe, so we thought we would include one way of making it here.

1 bottle red wine
150g/5oz sugar
Juice and grated peel of one small lemon
2 cardamom pods

4 cloves
2 bay leaves
2 cinnamon sticks

Place everything into a heavy-bottomed pan, stirring well in order to melt the sugar. Heat the mixture over a low heat, and leave to simmer for about an hour. Strain out the peel and spices, and serve in small mugs, with an optional shot of brandy, kirsch or other liqueur.

Pigeon and Walnut Pâté

2 plump pigeons
Butter for stuffing and frying
Salt and pepper, and cayenne pepper

1 bacon rasher, chopped
Shelled walnuts
1 tablespoon sherry or brandy

Stuff each pigeon with a lump of butter mixed with salt, pepper and a little cayenne pepper. Then brown the birds in a small saucepan with plenty of frothing butter, turning them frequently until all sides are browned. Add a chopped bacon rasher if you wish.

Now put them in a casserole, adding all the contents and juices from the pan. Add just one tablespoon of water before covering the casserole tightly with a sheet of foil and the lid. Cook at gas mark 4/180°C for 2 hours.

Take the pigeon flesh from the bones, weigh it, and add half its weight in shelled walnuts; then put the meat and nuts through the mincer – an old-fashioned mincer is better than an electric blender, which gives the finished pâté too fine a texture.

Combine about 55g/2oz softened butter with the minced mixture, and add a table-spoon of either sherry or brandy. Pack tightly into a terrine, and chill in the fridge.

Pigeon Tikka

It always pays to think 'out of the box' when trying to dream up new recipes! Here a tradi-tional rural meat is given an Indian twist. The quantities given will serve four as a main course, but bearing in mind the fact that a 'proper' tikka is normally served as a starter, it will obviously 'do' more when served as such. 'Lazy' garlic and ginger can be bought in jars from almost any supermarket and are a useful addition to the store cupboard.

1 teaspoon 'Lazy Garlic'
1 teaspoon 'Lazy Ginger'

1 teaspoon chilli powder
¼ teaspoon turmeric

1 teaspoon salt	1 tablespoon fresh coriander, finely chopped
150ml/5fl oz plain low fat yoghurt	450g/1lb pigeon breasts, skinned and cubed
4 tablespoons lemon juice	1 tablespoon vegetable oil

Mix together the garlic, ginger, chilli powder, turmeric, salt, yoghurt, lemon juice and coriander. Add the cubes of pigeon breasts and fold together well so that every piece of meat is coated with the mixture. Leave to marinate for at least a couple of hours.

Prepare a grill tray by lining it with foil (it makes washing up so much easier!), spoon in the pigeon meat mixture and level it to a single layer. Brush the oil over, and grill under a medium heat for 15–20 minutes, periodically turning and basting with more oil.

Garnish the dish with thinly sliced rings of onion, lemon slices and fresh coriander.

Pan-Fried Pigeon Breast with Creamed Potatoes, Celeriac and Rocket

For our book *The New Country Cook* (The Crowood Press, 2009) we visited the 'Cottage in the Wood', Malvern Wells, Worcestershire. This is a variation on one of their recipes.

200g/7oz potato, diced	Rocket salad
300g/10½oz celeriac, diced	Olive oil
200ml/7fl oz cream	Seasoning
1 teaspoon Dijon mustard	8 pigeon breasts

Cook the potatoes and celeriac together in a pan of boiling water for 4 minutes; drain and place in a hot oiled frying pan and fry for 1 minute. Add the cream and mustard, and simmer until the cream has reduced slightly.

Prepare the rocket salad by drizzling with oil, adding a pinch of salt and turning carefully so that each leaf is coated with oil.

When all is ready to serve, have ready a hot griddle pan, slightly oiled. Season the pigeon breasts and fry for approximately a minute on each side. Serve immediately.

Pan-Fried Woodpigeon, Celeriac Purée and Juniper Berries

Chris and Alison Davy have owned The Rose and Crown at Romaldkirk, Barnard Castle, Co. Durham, since 1989. As is the case with so many of these husband and wife teams, Chris is often behind the scenes in the kitchen whilst Alison is the perfect 'front of house' hostess and, from personal experience, looks after the customers and diners extremely well indeed. We are most grateful to them for allowing us to include this recipe here. As a point of interest, should you ever visit, be sure to seek out the collection of Bamforth's saucy postcards in the gentlemen's loos – Alison says, 'If we're not too busy, I sometimes take the ladies in to look at them!'

455g/16oz of celeriac	1 brace woodpigeon
A little cream, knob of butter, seasoning	150ml/5fl oz Madeira
for purée	90ml/3fl oz red wine

90ml/3fl oz port	2 tablespoons redcurrant jelly
6 juniper berries	Beef stock
2 bay leaves	85g/3oz unsalted butter, well chilled
Sprig fresh thyme	Heather sprig for garnish

Cook the celeriac in boiling salted water until soft, and then purée in a food processor adding a little cream and a knob of butter. Season to taste.

Heat a sauté pan with a little melted butter and oil. Sauté the pigeon breasts skin side down for 3 minutes; turn and cook the other side for the same time. Remove, season and keep warm.

Add the Madeira, red wine and port to the pan, together with the juniper berries, bay leaves, thyme and redcurrant jelly, and reduce by half. Add the stock and reduce by half again. Add the butter, and shake the pan to amalgamate well. Season.

Reheat the pigeon breasts, remove the skin, and slice on to the celeriac purée; strain the sauce over. Garnish with a sprig of heather – if you can find one!

Add the Madeira, red wine and port to the pan, together with the juniper berries, bay leaves, thyme and redcurrant jelly, and reduce by half.

Pan-Fried Woodpigeon, Celeriac Purée and Juniper Berries.

Reared Pigeon with Honey Sauce

Whilst there is no question that the taste of a reared pigeon is very different to that of a wild woodpigeon – the latter being far more variable depending upon what it has been eating – there is no reason why reared pigeon should not be used instead of wild pigeon in the recipes given in this chapter. Remember, however, that because reared pigeon are somewhat bigger than the average wild woodpigeon, it is important to take note of the fact that, if adapting recipes given elsewhere in this book, any cooking times may need to be slightly extended when dealing with commercially reared birds.

6 pigeons   Salt and pepper
4 dessertspoons corn oil

For the honey sauce

100ml/3fl oz corn oil	1 celery stick, trimmed and chopped
225g/8oz chicken pieces, chopped	1 carrot, peeled and chopped
60ml/2fl oz sherry vinegar	1 leek, washed and chopped
60ml/2 fl oz clear honey	1 bay leaf
3 shallots, peeled and finely chopped	1 sprig of fresh thyme
2 cloves garlic, peeled and finely chopped	1ltr/1¾ pint chicken stock

First deal with the pigeons: preheat the oven to 220°C/gas mark 7 and heat the oil in a roasting tin. When it is hot enough, season the pigeons, put them in the tin and brown them on all sides; roast for 10 minutes. Allow to rest, and when cool, carve them by first removing the legs and then the breasts. Place to one side, and finely chop the remainder of the carcass meat.

Make the sauce by heating half of the oil in a large saucepan, then add to it the chopped chicken and the remainder of the pigeon carcasses. Pour in the vinegar and bring to the boil. Add the honey and boil again.

Using the remainder of the oil from the sauce ingredients list, fry the shallots, garlic, celery, carrot and leek until golden in colour, and then add to the honey mixture. Stir well, then include the bay leaf, thyme and stock.

Bring back to the boil, whilst at the same time skimming off any 'froth' from the top of the mixture. Simmer for about an hour, then strain through a sieve and into another saucepan. Reduce the sauce to about two-thirds of its volume by boiling it for a further time.

Reheat the pigeon legs and breast in the oven for no more than 5 minutes (at the same temperature at which the birds were originally cooked). If necessary, bring the sauce back to the boil, and strain again before pouring it over the pigeon pieces which should by now have been plated up (use warm plates).

Bring to the table as quickly as possible.

Pigeon Breasts with Lemon and Honey

On our travels in connection with *The Pigeon Cook*, Philip and I were fortunate enough to come across 'Teesdale Game and Poultry' based in Barnard Castle, Co. Durham. A family business, it is now owned by Stephen Morrell; Stephen and his wife Alison have joined forces with professional writer Malcolm Pearce and produced *The Game and Cheese Book*, part of Malcolm's 'Easy Cook' series. Malcolm's other writings (author name Malcolm L. Pearce) cover a range of subjects including travel, leisure, history, politics and fiction. We are most grateful to him for allowing us to reproduce the following recipe in full:

> Allow two pigeon breasts per person, or three if you prefer.
> You will also need 40 grams (1¼ oz) butter, a tablespoon of
> chopped spring onions, the juice and zest of half a lemon,
> two teaspoons of runny honey, and salt and pepper for
> seasoning.

Heat the butter in a frying pan until it bubbles, and then add the pigeon breasts, which should have had their skins taken off. Fry these for four minutes each side at a high temperature. Towards the end put in the chopped spring onions. Add the honey, deglazing the pan with the liquid. Cook for a further two minutes. Take the pigeon breasts out, slice them thinly, and fan them out on a warm plate.

Return the pan to the heat and add the lemon juice and zest and reheat thoroughly. Season this to taste. Pour the sauce over the sliced pigeon breasts and serve immediately.

Roast Pigeons in a Bed of Garlic

Once roasted, garlic cloves lose their pungent flavour and instead become quite sweet and lovely to taste. However, owing to the number of cloves used in this recipe, it still might be inadvisable to attempt much kissing immediately afterwards!

4 pigeons

2 sticks celery, finely chopped

2 sprigs of rosemary (with the leaves stripped from the stalk)

4 sprigs each of thyme and parsley (strip two of each, leaving the other two intact)

20 garlic cloves, clean but unpeeled

2 tablespoons olive oil

1 carrot, chopped into thick chunks

2 shallots, peeled and cut in half

1 large wine glass of white wine

Make a rough stuffing of one stick of celery, the rosemary and the stripped thyme and parsley: take four of the cloves, and pack these and the stuffing into the body of each pigeon. Use a pastry brush to coat the breasts of the birds with oil.

In the bottom of a large casserole, spread half-a-dozen garlic cloves, the remaining celery stick, the sprigs of thyme and parsley and the carrot and shallots. Place the pigeons on top of this and pack round with the rest of the garlic cloves (use more than stated if you wish – or dare!).

Add the rest of the oil and the white wine, then cover tightly with a lid and cook at gas mark 6/400°C for about 45 minutes to 1 hour (check periodically, remembering that because the birds are laid close together, plus the fact that they are stuffed, may mean that the cooking time needs to be increased).

At the end of cooking it is probably easiest for your diners if you were to remove the breasts from each bird, rather than presenting them with the whole thing on their plate. Alternatively you could halve each one before serving.

Pour the juices left over from cooking into a small pan, and cook on the hob for a couple of minutes in order to reduce and therefore thicken the liquid. Save the garlic cloves from the casserole, and arrange on or around the pigeon. Finally top off with the sauce from the pan.

A LABOUR-SAVING ROASTING TIP

The basic method for roasting all game birds is to put butter inside and out, season, and cover with strips of bacon. It also helps to place a peeled apple in the body cavity. Despite all this, they should still be basted frequently during cooking. Save labour (and washing-up!) by preparing pigeons as above and placing them into roasting bags or tightly closed foil parcels – then they'll baste themselves. Start cooking by laying the birds on one side of their breast, turning them to the other side halfway through. Turn them right side up when nearly done, and open the roasting bag or foil if you wish them to brown.

Roast Woodpigeon with Potato and Beetroot Rosti, Calvelo Nero, Beetroot and Twice-Cooked Jerusalem Artichoke

The Old Bridge at Huntingdon is wonderfully run by owner John Hoskins, his wife Julia and general manager Nina Beamond. Situated on the outskirts of town, it's not immedi-

The Old Bridge Beetroot Rosti.

ately the place one would think of as having both rabbit and pigeon recipes on the menu – but it does, and excellent they are, too! Many thanks to John, Nina and head chef Simon Cadge not only for looking after us so well during our visit, but also for allowing us to include this particular recipe.

2 large beetroot
3 Jerusalem artichokes (if small)
1 medium potato
1 banana shallot
1 clove garlic

Chicken stock (sufficient to make a paste)
1 stem calvelo nero (black cabbage)
2 whole woodpigeons
Butter (lots!)

Tinfoil one beetroot and all the Jerusalem artichokes and roast for 45 minutes at gas mark 4/180°C.

Grate the potato and the other beetroot, and thinly slice the shallot and garlic. Heat up a large knob of butter in a small pan. Add the potato/beetroot mix, and press it down firmly so that the butter goes all the way through. Cook slowly on each side for 6–8 minutes, or until the rosti is crispy on both sides.

With a hand (stick) blender, make a beetroot purée with the roasted beetroot, a knob of butter and chicken stock. Peel the artichokes and pan-fry in butter until golden.

Destalk the calvelo nero, blanch, and reheat in butter (deep fry some for garnish if you like.)

Roast Woodpigeon with Potato and Beetroot Rosti, Calvelo Nero, Beetroot and Twice-cooked Jerusalem Artichoke.

Pan-fry the pigeons in butter until golden all round, and then roast for 8–10 minutes at gas mark 6/200°C; 'rest' for 10 minutes. Remove the breasts and set aside to keep warm.

Use a quality red wine sauce to pour over (a good tip to obtain a 'gamey' flavour is to rough chop the pigeon bones and simmer in the sauce for 10 minutes).

Tipsy Pigeon

This is a really old recipe, which has been adapted for modern-day use from a game recipe book published in the late 1890s.

16 black olives	8 slices garlic sausage
125ml/4fl oz dry sherry	100g/3½oz flour
4 pigeons, plucked and drawn	600ml/1pt chicken stock
60ml/2fl oz olive oil	60ml/2fl oz brandy
2 large onions, peeled and sliced	Salt and pepper
225g/8oz bacon, rinded and chopped	

Marinate the olives in the sherry for 2 hours. Fry the pigeons in the oil until golden brown – about 5 minutes. Remove from the pan with a slotted spoon and put in a casserole.

Fry the onions, bacon and garlic sausage in the remaining fat until brown – another 5 minutes. Remove from the pan (again with a slotted spoon) and add to the casserole, together with the sherry and infused olives.

Gradually stir the flour into the fat remaining in the frying pan, and cook for a couple of minutes (note that you may not require exactly the amount of flour quoted). Now carefully stir in the stock, bring to the boil, and stir until such time as the sauce thickens. Finally add the brandy and seasoning.

Pour the sauce over the pigeons, cover, and cook in the oven at gas mark 3/170°C for about 1½ hours, or until the pigeons are tender.

Russian Pigeon

Carrying on with the alcohol theme (see Tipsy Pigeon above, among others), here's a recipe that uses vodka – hence the 'Russian' part of the title, we suppose; some might be pleased to know that gin can be used instead of vodka. Either way, it is quite a quick meal to prepare; and for something a little different in the way of an accompaniment, try serving it with buttered noodles.

8 woodpigeon breasts, or 4 from table-bred pigeons	150ml/5fl oz chicken or vegetable stock
55g/2oz butter	150ml/5fl oz soured cream
115g/4oz sliced button mushrooms	Salt and pepper
1½ tablespoons flour	2–3 tablespoons vodka (or gin)

Brown the pigeon breasts in the butter (taking care not to let the butter burn, otherwise the whole dish will be ruined), then put them in a warmed, shallow casserole dish. Put aside, but keep hot.

In the same pan as the breasts have been fried, gently fry the mushrooms; then remove them with a slotted spoon and place them over the breasts.

Carefully add the flour to the frying pan, and slowly stir in the stock with a wooden spoon. Cook over a gentle heat until a sauce is formed. Remove from the heat and allow to cool slightly before adding the cream.

Season, and turn in the vodka or gin; then tip the contents of the pan over the pigeon/mushroom mix. If you like, dust with a pinch of paprika for a little colour and 'spiciness'.

Simple Ways with Young Pigeons

Really young, tender birds can be cooked by either grilling or shallow frying in butter. Prepare them in the following way:

Remove the breasts from the carcass and cut each into two long pieces. Make an incision in each, and stuff with chopped cooked mushrooms. Dip the breast pieces into whisked egg, followed by breadcrumbs, and cover with melted butter. Grill carefully until thoroughly cooked, or shallow fry in butter. Either way is perfect when served with a summer salad.

Breadcrumbed pigeon breasts served with a summer salad.

Braised Pigeon with Orange

It is surprising just how many game recipes are associated with oranges. Duck is a classic and obvious one, but the citrus effect also works well with pigeons.

4 pigeons	150ml/5fl oz port or red wine
4 small oranges	300ml/10fl oz stock
4 rashers bacon	Salt and pepper
55g/2oz butter	1 bouquet garni
4 shallots, chopped	½ teaspoon crushed coriander
1 tablespoon flour	2 tablespoons Cointreau

With a potato peeler, remove some thin slices of zest from half the oranges, and put to one side. Place an orange in the cavity of each pigeon, and wrap a rasher of bacon around each bird, 'pinning' it in place with a wooden cocktail stick.

Heat the butter in a large casserole, and fry each pigeon until it is golden brown. Put the birds to one side, and fry the shallots in the same pan. When they are also golden brown, stir in the flour and cook for 3 minutes, then gradually stir in the wine, stock and seasoning.

Return the pigeons to the casserole, and add the bouquet garni and the coriander. Cover and cook in the oven at 170°C/gas mark 3 for 1½–2 hours, or until the pigeons are tender.

As the pigeons are cooking, cut the orange zest into strips, place in a small pan with a little water and simmer gently for 15–20 minutes. Strain and reserve the strips.

Once the pigeons are cooked, transfer them to a serving dish. Strain the sauce and juices from the casserole into a saucepan – if necessary, thicken the sauce with the smallest amount of cornflour, remembering to stir constantly as you do so, otherwise you may end up with lumps.

Assuming all is well, add the Cointreau to the sauce, then pour it all over the pigeons. Sprinkle the orange strips over the birds, and serve immediately.

Pigeons à la Française

Almost every recipe book that deals with game cooking includes a dish named 'Pigeons à la Française' – and every one is different! This is our 'take' on an old classic.

4 pigeons	175g/6oz button mushrooms
Salt and pepper	1 lettuce, washed and shredded
4 tablespoons cooking oil	450g/1lb frozen minted *petits pois*
6 tablespoons dry sherry	

To make the beurre manié

15g/½oz butter	2 teaspoons cornflour

Halve the pigeons, and season with the salt and pepper. Seal them by frying in the cooking oil. Place in a casserole dish and add the sherry and mushrooms, then cover and cook at gas mark 3/170°C for about 1½ hours. After an hour into cooking, add the lettuce and minted peas.

Thicken the juices into a sauce by creaming together the butter and cornflour (the *beurre manié*), and adding a little at a time. Serve from the casserole dish accompanied by any of the suggestions to be found in the next chapter, 'Stuffings and Accompaniments'.

Barbecued Pigeon Pieces with Saffron and Yoghurt

As you will only be using pigeon breasts cut into chunks suitable for skewering and barbecuing, this particular recipe can be quite wasteful of pigeon (although the remainder of the carcass can be used to make excellent stock). As a very rough guide, allow two pigeon breasts per person: this recipe will suffice for two people – for bigger numbers, use more pigeon breasts and increase the quantities of the other ingredients accordingly.

4 pigeon breasts, cut into pieces suitable for barbecuing
Plain yoghurt (enough to pour over and cover the pigeon pieces)

1 medium-sized onion, finely chopped
3 tablespoons lemon juice
A dash of soy sauce
¼ teaspoon saffron

In a bowl large enough to hold them, marinate the pigeon pieces in the yoghurt, onion, lemon juice, soy sauce and saffron (as saffron doesn't mix evenly with the yogurt, the best way is to soak it in half an egg-cup of very hot water for 10–15 minutes before adding it to the marinade, water and all). Cover, and leave in the fridge overnight.

Barbecue pigeon pieces kebab-style.

Remove the pigeon chunks from the marinade, skewer, brush with olive oil or melted butter and cook over a very hot barbecue. Cook until they are very slightly blackened round the edges, and cooked through to the middle. Serve with Basmati rice and skewered vegetables such as courgette and button mushrooms brushed with the remainder of the yoghurt marinade and also cooked over the barbecue.

Spanish-Style Pigeon

Pigeon dishes are very popular in Spain – to be truly authentic, braise some extra onions to serve round the plate, and offer wedges of sour dough bread to your guests.

4 whole pigeons	2 tomatoes, skinned and chopped
Olive oil for basting and sautéing	1 bay leaf
Salt and pepper to season	125ml/4fl oz brandy
1 medium onion, rough chopped	250ml/8oz dry white wine
1 stick celery, rough chopped	225–350g/8–12oz mushrooms
2 carrots, rough chopped	

Place the pigeons into a large roasting pan or casserole dish, baste with olive oil and season with salt and pepper. Oven cook at gas mark 6/200°C until the birds begin to brown, and then arrange the chopped vegetables and bay leaf around them. Return the dish to the oven to roast for another 10 minutes.

Take the dish out of the oven and pour in the wine and brandy (if necessary add water until the liquid completely covers the bottom of the roasting pan). Lower the oven temperature to gas mark 4/180°C, and continue to roast for about 1½ hours, periodically turning the pigeons from back to breast, and back again.

While the birds are roasting, wash the mushrooms and trim the stems as needed. Pat dry with kitchen towel, and sauté in a frying pan for about 5 minutes.

Transfer the pigeons to a serving plate, together with some of the vegetables and residual juices. Spoon over the fried mushrooms and serve immediately, accompanied by green vegetables and game chips.

GRILLED PIGEON

Young tender pigeons can be grilled if they are kept well basted. Place a small knob of butter inside the carcass and brush the breasts with melted butter, then cook under a moderately hot grill, occasionally coating with more butter. For the final 5 minutes of cooking time add sections of grapefruit, and garnish with cherries and lettuce before taking to the table.

To grill just the breasts, smear with butter and seasoning and cook under a hot heat for 5–10 minutes. For grilling either whole birds or breasts, experiment by marinating in a mixture of port, red wine, raisins, oil, fresh orange juice and zest.

Quick and Easy Pigeon Cannelloni

The use of pre-packaged ingredients may cause this particular recipe to be frowned on by the cooking police, but it's a quick and tasty way of using up pigeon breasts that may otherwise linger in the freezer.

250g/9oz packet frozen chopped spinach
1 small onion, finely chopped
30g/1oz butter
250g/9oz minced pigeon breasts
130g tin sweetcorn, drained
130g tin diced capsicum, drained

2 tablespoons dried breadcrumbs
1 beaten egg
250ml jar spaghetti sauce
120g packet instant cannelloni shells
140g jar cream cheese spread

Gently cook the spinach, onion and butter in a small frying pan for 10 minutes. Pour into a bowl and allow to cool.

Using the same pan, add a little olive oil and cook the minced pigeon breasts for 3 minutes. Into the cooled spinach mix add the mince, sweetcorn, capsicum, breadcrumbs and egg.

Spread some of the spaghetti sauce over the base of a shallow casserole dish. Spoon the filling mixture into the cannelloni shells and arrange them on top of the spaghetti sauce. Pour the remaining sauce over, and dot with teaspoonfuls of cheese spread.

Bake at gas mark 4/180°C for 40 minutes. Leave to stand in a warm place for 5 minutes before serving.

Carpaccio of Essex Woodpigeon

The Bell at Horndon-on-the-Hill, Essex, is a wonderful 500-year-old building; it was first used in the Middle Ages by pilgrims and wool merchants who would stay there until low water when they could cross the river and continue on their journey. Today it is owned by Christine and John Vereker, and many of its characterful bedrooms have a nautical/Lord Nelson feel about them – due no doubt to John's naval career. Joanne Butler is the general manager, and she did much to make our visit to The Bell so perfect. Stuart Fry is the head chef, and he is in charge of eleven others; in some weeks they provide tasty dishes for as many as 800 covers, which is no mean feat! (As well as this recipe, Stuart was, with the aid of Stephen Treadwell, kind enough to supply us with his award-winning recipe 'Wild Rabbit Saddle in Herb Mousse with Fondant Potato' and 'Rabbit Leg Ballotine and Wild Mushrooms', which appears in our book The Rabbit Cook, also published by The Crowood Press.)

As with many country pubs and restaurants, all the game, pigeons and rabbits used at the Bell are locally sourced.

10 pigeons, plucked, drawn and on the bone
15g/½oz sea salt
150ml/5fl oz balsamic vinegar
5 tablespoons soy sauce
5 teaspoons Worcestershire sauce
4 cloves garlic

1 bunch basil
½ bunch thyme
15 black peppercorns
300ml/10fl oz dry white wine
600ml/20fl oz olive oil

Carpaccio of Essex Woodpigeon.

Remove the wishbone from the pigeons and take off the breasts. Slice off the skin and remove any breast sinew, then put to one side. Place all the other ingredients into a pan and heat gently (it is important not to allow it to boil, says Stuart) on a stove.

In a hot frying pan, seal the breasts and place them into this marinade, making sure that all the breasts are completely submerged in the liquid. Leave to cool for at least 3 to 4 hours, or better still, overnight in the fridge.

To serve, remove the breasts from the marinade and slice thinly lengthways. Lay on a plate, together with Puy lentils, mustard vinaigrette and rings of shallots for garnish.

Pigeon in Minutes

This recipe is so quick and simple it really can be made in minutes. See the box on page 21 for ideas on possible marinades.

4 pigeon breasts, marinated and cut into long, thin strips	115g/4oz mushrooms
2 red onions, sliced	55g/2oz butter
	150ml/5floz crème fraîche

Soften the onions in butter, add the pigeon breasts and cook gently. Add the mushrooms and half the marinade. Cook gently again before finally adding the crème fraîche. Stir and serve with rice. (When cooking rice, add a little oil to the water and fluff up with a fork immediately before serving.)

Pigeon in Minutes.

Pigeon Breasts in a Wild Mushroom Sauce

We featured this recipe from the highly successful 'Game's On' campaign in *Cook Game* (The Crowood Press, 2008), and according to those who have since tried it, it has been a huge success.

4 pigeons
½ onion, chopped
1 carrot, chopped
1 stick celery, chopped
1 tablespoon tomato purée
1 miniature bottle brandy

600ml/1pint chicken stock
Bay leaf and thyme
Olive oil
Seasoning
225g/8oz wild mushrooms

Remove the breasts from the pigeons and put to one side. Roughly chop the remains of the carcass and legs, and fry quickly in a hot frying pan together with all the chopped vegetables until brown. Add the tomato purée and cook for a further 2 minutes. Add the brandy and flame. Add the chicken stock and herbs, simmer and reduce the volume by two-thirds. Strain and season, then put aside to keep warm.

Sauté the pigeon breasts in a little oil – both sides should be well done whilst the centre remains slightly 'pink' – and leave to rest on a warm serving dish. Add a little more oil to the same pan and quickly fry the washed and seasoned mushrooms until brown. Cover the breasts with sauce and wild mushrooms, and serve immediately.

Roast Woodpigeon, Pickled Beetroot, Beetroot Purée and Horseradish Cream

Lawrence and Julia Murphy own Fat Olives in South Street, in Emsworth, Hampshire, and quite often have this dish on their evening menu – and very popular it is, too!

8 woodpigeon breasts, with the skin and membrane removed
8 sprigs of thyme

4 peppercorns
2 cloves of garlic, sliced
Olive oil

Place the pigeon breasts into a container with the thyme, peppercorns and garlic. Cover with olive oil and leave in a fridge overnight.

For the pickled beetroot
1 beetroot
125ml/4fl oz water
55g/2oz sugar

60ml/2fl oz white wine vinegar
1 bay leaf
3 peppercorns

Peel the beetroot using a potato peeler. Slice, and place the slices into a container. Bring all the other ingredients to the boil. Taste, and adjust the seasoning. Pour the liquid, still hot, over the slices of beetroot and allow to cool.

For the beetroot purée
2 shallots
Butter for cooking
1 beetroot

85ml/3fl oz double cream
Seasoning
Splash of white wine

Finely dice the shallots and sweat in butter. Add the peeled, diced beetroot and a little water. Put a lid on the pan and heat until just cooked. Add the double cream, seasoning and wine. Remove the lid and reduce by half. Liquidize and push through a sieve. Keep warm.

For the horseradish cream
30g/1oz grated horseradish
85ml/3fl oz double cream

Seasoning

Put the cream, horseradish and seasoning into a bowl and whisk until thick. Refrigerate.

To assemble the dish, remove the pigeons from the marinade, season, and pan-fry until brown. Place in a hot oven for 4 minutes. Remove, and allow to rest for a further 4 minutes. Sprinkle with sea salt.

Place a spoon of purée in the bottom of a serving bowl, and top with some drained, pickled beetroot. Place the roasted pigeon on top of this. Finally quenelle the horseradish cream, and place on top of the breasts.

'Then' says Julia, 'serve quickly before the cream melts!'

Roast Woodpigeon, Pickled Beetroot, Beetroot Purée and Horseradish Cream.

Casserole of Pigeons

The great thing about casserole cooking is the fact that all the preparation can be done in advance, because everything is more or less in one pot, there is very little washing up of coated pots and pans, and perhaps most importantly, the slow cooking involved means that every possible ounce of goodness is kept and savoured. Simple but effective, no wonder so many recipes involve the use of a casserole dish.

115g/4oz mushrooms
2 large tomatoes
4 tablespoons beef dripping
4 pigeons
2 tablespoons flour

150ml/5fl oz beef stock
Salt and pepper
2 tablespoons claret wine
Glacé cherries and croûtons for garnish

Peel the mushrooms and skin and slice the tomatoes. Heat the dripping in a frying pan and brown the pigeons before placing them into a large casserole. Toss the mushrooms, then the tomato slices in the dripping.

Blend the flour with the stock, add to the mushroom mixture and, stirring continuously, slowly bring to the boil. Season to taste and add the wine. Pour over the pigeons, cover and cook at gas mark 4/180°C for approximately 1½ hours.

Serve garnished with the cherries and croûtons.

Pigeon Breast and Sausage Stuffing 'Sandwich'

A sandwich without bread – unless you count the fresh breadcrumbs used in the sausage stuffing! In fact it's not really a sandwich at all, and gets its name from the way the breasts are placed together: it is actually more suited to a dinner party than a picnic.

8 woodpigeon breasts
115g/4oz sausagemeat
1 onion, peeled and finely chopped
Pinch dried sage
15g/½oz fresh breadcrumbs
1 tablespoon of flour, plus a little extra
    for dusting a work board
4 rashers of bacon, with any rind removed

100g/3½oz butter
55g/2oz mushrooms, wiped and sliced
1 x 115g/4oz tin chestnuts, peeled and
    chopped
1 tablespoon sherry or brandy
150ml/5fl oz chicken or vegetable stock
60ml/2fl oz cream

Make a stuffing by mixing together the sausagemeat, half of the chopped onion, the sage and the breadcrumbs; mix well. Divide the stuffing into four balls, which should then be gently rolled into slightly flattened sausage shapes (roughly the length of your pigeon breasts) on a floured work surface or board. Wrap a slice of bacon round each one.

Melt two-thirds of the butter in a frying pan and fry the 'sausages' until the bacon is browned.

Take two pigeon breasts and place a sausage in between them and gently press together. To make the sandwich keep together whilst cooking, either tie the breasts with thin butcher's string, or (and probably the easiest option!) skewer them together with a couple of cocktail sticks. Repeat the process with the other breasts and fillings.

As best you can, coat or roll them in flour, and fry slowly in the residue left in the pan until they are cooked through without becoming dried out. Put in an ovenproof serving dish, remove the skewers or string and keep them hot.

In the same frying pan, add the remainder of the butter, the remaining half onion, the mushrooms and the chestnuts. When tender, stir in the tablespoon of flour, the alcohol, stock and cream. Stirring continually, heat until the sauce thickens, then pour it immediately over the hot pigeon breast 'sandwiches' and take straight to the table.

MAKING FRESH BREADCRUMBS

Breadcrumbs are sometimes required (as in the recipe for Pigeon Breast and Sausage Stuffing 'Sandwich') and can be made quite quickly. Cut off the crusts from a piece of half stale white bread; dice it, add a spoonful of flour, and process in a food blender. Alternatively, do as before and place the bread and flour in a cloth: gather up the edges, and crush the bread with the flat of your hand before rubbing the mix through a mesh sieve.

Pigeon Enchiladas

4 pigeon breasts, skinned
Olive oil for frying
400g/14oz tin tomatoes
½ Spanish onion
2 cloves garlic
2 teaspoons chilli powder
1 teaspoon dried marjoram
300ml/10fl oz stock

Salt and pepper
8 soft flour tortillas
½ lettuce
2 spring onions
85g/3oz feta cheese
1 red onion
3 sprigs coriander
1 lime

Cut the pigeon breasts into strips and stir-fry for 5 minutes in two tablespoons of olive oil. Using a slotted spoon, remove the pigeon strips from the pan and keep warm.

Drain the tomatoes. Peel and finely chop the Spanish onion and garlic. Add a further tablespoon of oil to the pan used for the pigeon, and fry the onion and garlic for 3 minutes. Add the tomatoes, chilli powder, marjoram and stock, and bring to the boil. Continue boiling for 15 minutes or until the sauce has reduced by roughly a third. Season to taste.

Wrap the tortillas in foil, and bake at gas mark 4/180°C for 10 minutes. Meanwhile, shred the lettuce and spring onions. Dice the feta cheese, then peel and finely slice the red onion.

Brush one side of each tortilla with the sauce, and scatter the lettuce and pigeon on top. Roll up the tortillas and arrange on a serving plate. Spoon over the remaining sauce, and scatter the cheese and red onion strands over the tortillas. Garnish with coriander, and the lime cut into wedges.

Pigeon Enchiladas.

Pigeon with Tomato and Chocolate Sauce

An unusual combination one must admit, but it is surprising how often chocolate is used in game-inspired recipes . . . partridge and hare spring immediately to mind.

4 pigeons
4 rashers bacon, chopped
2 large onions, sliced
2 carrots, diced
2 cloves garlic, crushed
1 tablespoon chopped parsley
Salt and pepper

Nutmeg, grated
1 tablespoon red wine vinegar
Beef or game stock
2 beef tomatoes, skinned and chopped
1 glass dry sherry
2–3 teaspoons grated bitter chocolate

Brown the pigeons and bacon in a little oil, then place them, breast down, in a flame-resistant casserole dish. Spoon in the onions and add the carrots, garlic, parsley, tomatoes, seasoning and a little grated nutmeg. Add the vinegar and just enough stock to cover.

Bring to the boil, then cover the casserole dish and simmer until the pigeon breasts feel tender when poked with the point of a sharp knife. Remove the breasts and keep warm.

Blend the sauce in a liquidizer and bring back to the heat, very slowly adding the sherry and the grated chocolate. Simmer for a further 10 minutes, stirring frequently.

On individual serving plates lay a bed of buttered noodles, and place two pigeon breasts on each. Finish off by pouring the sauce over the breasts.

Pigeon 'Scampi'

Jeremy's wife Melinda 'invented' the basics of this recipe a long time ago, and it has been adapted here to include pigeon breasts.

3 shallots, peeled and sliced
Bouquet garni
1 glass dry white wine
55g/2oz butter
Flour
1 garlic clove, peeled and crushed

1 teaspoon concentrated tomato purée
250ml/8fl oz stock
450g/1lb pigeon breasts cut into long, thin strips
115g/4oz mushrooms, wiped and sliced
3 tomatoes, skinned and sliced

Simmer the shallots and the bouquet garni with the wine until the mixture has reduced by half. Remove the bouquet garni.

In another pan, melt half the butter, add 30g/1oz flour and stir into a roux before adding the garlic, tomato purée and stock. Simmer for 5–10 minutes. Pour in the wine mixture, and cook for a further 5 minutes.

Meanwhile, roll the pigeon pieces in flour and sauté in the remaining butter for 5 minutes, tossing frequently. Sauté the mushrooms and add to the sauce, together with the tomatoes. Reheat the sauce for a minute or two, and spoon over the pigeon 'scampi'.

Serve over a bed of rice or noodles.

Hungarian Pigeon Soup with Pickled Gherkins and Soured Cream

This is more of a stew than a soup, and is perfect for the winter – to make it even more substantial, try adding tinned butter beans or small dumplings.

225g/8oz pigeon breasts, minced
115g/4oz onion, chopped
30g/1oz butter
350g/12oz potato, diced
225g/8oz tin tomatoes

850ml/1½ pint stock
Seasoning
2 cloves garlic, peeled and crushed
4–6 pickled gherkins, sliced
Soured cream

Fry the chopped onion and minced pigeon breasts in the butter until lightly browned. Add the diced potato and fry for a further 2–3 minutes.

Stir in the canned tomatoes, the stock, seasoning and garlic. Simmer gently for 30 minutes, then add the sliced pickled gherkins. Heat for a further minute or so, then ladle the soup into bowls and add a swirl of soured cream.

Serve with warm, crusty bread and a glass or two of medium-heavy red wine.

Stuffed Pigeon

As with the 'Pigeon with Warmed Mushroom Salad' (see below, p. 62), this recipe requires whole pigeons rather than merely using the breasts.

Hungarian Pigeon Soup.

4 pigeons (retain their livers if the birds are being specially prepared for this dish)
4 rashers streaky bacon
1 tablespoon flour

2 tablespoons white wine
1 tablespoon tomato purée
1 tablespoon Cognac
2 tablespoons olive oil

For the stuffing
1 large slice stale white bread, broken into crumbs
4 tablespoons sausagemeat
1 clove garlic, crushed
2 sprigs parsley

2 eggs, beaten
Nutmeg, grated
Seasoning

Prepare the stuffing by mixing together the breadcrumbs, the crushed livers from the pigeons, the sausagemeat, garlic and sprigs of parsley. Add the eggs, nutmeg and seasoning, and mix well for a second time before dividing the mixture and stuffing the insides of each bird.

Put a rasher of bacon over the breast of each bird. Place the pigeons in a casserole dish, sprinkle with the flour, and moisten with the white wine, olive oil, Cognac, the tomato purée and about half a glass of water. Place in a moderate oven for around 45 minutes.

When cooked, remove the birds and keep warm – they can be served whole or in halves, or serve just the breasts; if choosing the latter method, remember to include a spoonful of the stuffing with each serving.

Deglaze the casserole dish by adding a little more water or wine to the sauce residue, heat and stir until it is of a good consistency, and pour over the birds before serving.

'MACBETH'S PIGEON'

Sue Gibson of Macbeth's game dealers, Moray, Scotland told us that the following method is a great way of using up old grouse, but we see no reason why it shouldn't work equally as well with pigeon breasts. Sue says that 'it's more a way of cooking than an actual recipe, but it is brilliant!'

Take the breasts from a pigeon and slice them horizontally so you have thin pieces of meat. Allow one breast per person for a starter and two for a main. Melt enough good quality butter in a deepish dish and perhaps add some extra flavouring such as thyme, sage or garlic – or all three! Place the pigeon pieces in the butter, and poach very gently in a warm oven until just cooked, moving the pieces around half way through to enable even cooking. The butter must not boil, or the meat will toughen. Cooking will take around 30 minutes depending on quantities.

The meat is delicious served warm with celeriac remoulade, beetroot, or as a warm salad with some blueberries or redcurrants.

Pigeons with Cherries in Eau-de-Vie

Otherwise known as 'Pigeon aux Cerises et à l'Eau-de-vie', this is a quick, simple and very tasty recipe.

4 pigeons
Salt
Pepper, freshly ground
85g/3oz butter

Eau-de-vie (or cherry brandy)
680g/1½lb firm cherries, washed and
    destoned

After plucking and dressing the birds, remove the heads, feet and wingtips. Salt and pepper the pigeons, then put 55g/2oz of the butter into a *cocotte* (casserole dish) and brown them thoroughly on all sides. Add a tablespoon or two of eau-de-vie (or cherry brandy), and the main bulk of the cherries – keep back around twenty of the cherries for the final presentation.

Cover the dish and leave to simmer for about 15 minutes, turning the pigeons mid-way through. Take the birds from the casserole, cut each into two, and keep somewhere warm.

On the heat, deglaze the dish with another tablespoon of eau-de-vie and the remainder of the butter. Adjust the seasoning by adding a little more freshly milled pepper. Add the cherries previously held back; cover the sauce and the cherries and leave for 5 minutes more.

Place the half-pigeons on to a serving plate, and spoon over the cherries and amalgamated cooking juices; finally decorate with five cherries still with the stalks attached.

Apparently a bottle of Beaujolais Cru, such as St Amour, goes exceptionally well with this particular French dish.

Mustard-Grilled Pigeon with Poppy Seeds

8 pigeon breasts
2 tablespoons poppy seeds

Any of the marinade suggestions given elsewhere can be used for this recipe – alternatively you could try the following:

1 tablespoon mustard
4 tablespoons olive oil
4 tablespoons cranberry juice

½ teaspoon 'Lazy Garlic'
A little salt and pepper

Mix together, and marinate the pigeon breasts in a clingfilm-covered bowl overnight in the fridge.

For the mustard sauce
300ml/10fl oz mild mustard
55g/2oz brown sugar
60ml/20fl oz cranberry juice

2 teaspoons fresh tarragon, finely chopped
Salt and pepper

Mix together all the ingredients and set aside.

Pre-heat the grill to medium and cook the pigeon breasts for about 20 minutes, turning them over frequently and brushing them as necessary (and liberally) with the mustard sauce about 5 minutes into cooking. Baste more frequently as the end of cooking time approaches, and 5 minutes before it does, sprinkle the pigeon breasts with the poppy seeds.

Remove the breasts and cut into oblique slices, then arrange on a serving plate and pour over the juices from the bottom of the grill pan. Heat up any unused mustard sauce, and serve separately in a small jug or sauceboat.

Pigeon Stir-Fry

Minced pigeon breasts make a good alternative to minced beef when it comes to cooking chilli dishes or making burgers – or, when cut into thin strips, a great stir-fry. Place a little oil in a wok or large frying pan, and cook the meat for a minute (turning frequently) before adding any combination of finely sliced ginger, spring onions, peppers and any other stir-fry choice of vegetables. The important thing with a stir-fry is, as the name suggests, to stir constantly as the food cooks, and not leave it on the heat until it loses its crispness.

Pigeon Stir-Fry.

Pigeon Salad with Bacon and Blackberry Vinaigrette

James Rogers, co-proprietor of The Dog at Grundisburgh, Suffolk, says that his love of cooking 'started at a young age, with visits to my grandparents in Northumberland, where we regularly enjoyed eating wild game. As a kid growing up, it was not uncommon to find a brace of pigeon, pheasant or a couple of trout hanging on the door handle when returning from school.'

James has since attracted industry-wide recognition and has won a string of awards for his cooking. The Dog (which he co-owns with his brother Charles) has been awarded the title of East Anglia's Best Gastropub at the Great British Pub Awards, and numerous 'Food Excellence' certificates adorn the walls inside. James was kind enough to supply the following recipe:

4 woodpigeons (8 breasts!)
4 rashers smoked streaky bacon, cut to
    lardons
Fresh salad (James uses a mix of endive,
    lollo rosso, radicchio and oak leaf),
    together with blanched green beans

Blackberry vinegar
Fresh chives
A few croûtons

Remove the pigeon from the bone, place in a smoking hot pan and cook for 45 seconds on each side. Season and place in a hot oven for 1 minute, remove and rest for

Pigeon Salad with Bacon and Blackberry Vinaigrette.

45 minutes ('They should be rare/medium rare,' says James). Remove the pigeon from the pan, and fry the bacon lardons in the pan juices.

Arrange the leaves and beans on the plate as desired, slice the pigeon and place on the salad, sprinkle on the bacon. Add the blackberry vinaigrette to the pan, deglaze, and then dress the salad with this reduction; finish with chives and croutons.

NB: To make blackberry vinegar, de-stalk 450g (1lb) blackberries. Place the berries into the bottom of an earthernware dish to a depth of around 5cm (2in) and add enough cider vinegar to cover. Seal the dish with clingfilm and leave for 3–5 days before straining the mixture through a muslin bag. Then, in a pan, for every 300ml (½pt) of liquid made, place 225g (8oz) sugar and add the liquid. Bring to the boil and simmer for five minutes. Cool and bottle until needed.

Pigeon with Warmed Mushroom Salad

For this recipe you do need whole pigeons, plucked and dressed.

2 pigeons	1 teaspoon mustard
Butter (enough to smear the breasts)	1 teaspoon Worcester sauce
Seasoning	1 teaspoon mushroom ketchup
115g/4oz cheese, finely grated	1 tablespoon brown sugar
150ml/5fl oz stock	2 tablespoons port

Season the pigeons well and smear with butter. Lay them in a roasting tin and place in the oven at gas mark 7/220°C for 20 minutes. Afterwards, cut each pigeon in half lengthways and place in a casserole. Sprinkle with cheese and moisten with stock, then cover, and cook at gas mark 3/160°C for 45 minutes.

Meanwhile mix together the mustard, Worcester sauce, brown sugar, mushroom ketchup and port. When the pigeon halves are cooked, transfer them to a serving plate. Pour the mixed sauce ingredients into the casserole and bring to the boil before pouring over the birds.

For the warmed mushroom salad

2 tablespoons oil	Seasoning
1 medium onion, finely chopped	55g/2oz each of oyster mushrooms, shiitake,
1 garlic clove, peeled and chopped	enoki and one other of your choice
2 red chillies, deseeded and sliced	2 teaspoons toasted sesame seeds
1 large flat or field mushroom, wiped and sliced	A few leaves of flat parsley

Heat the oil in a pan and fry the onion, garlic and chillies until they are soft but not discoloured. Add the sliced flat mushroom, season, and mix together gently before adding the selection of exotic mushrooms and cooking until tender. Serve with the pigeon, having first sprinkled the mushrooms with toasted sesame seeds and garnished with the parsley leaves.

Juniper-Marinated Pigeon Breast with Radish Salad

This recipe, from the menu at The Bell, Skenfrith, Monmouthshire, uses locally sourced pigeon combined with vegetables and fruit from their own organic kitchen garden. The Bell was reopened by Janet and William Hutchings in 2001. They have converted to organic/biodynamic status in the garden, which, as Janet says, 'just means you have to be one step ahead of the bug and insect life!' They now supply all their own salad crops, feves, chard and baby vegetables as well as herbs and some soft fruits. Both Janet and William are very conscious of 'food miles', and source all other produce from as close to The Bell as possible. They are also members of the 'slow food movement'.

This particular recipe from them is intended as a 'starter'.

4 pigeon breasts	250g/9oz mixed salad leaves
4 fresh figs	6 long French radishes

Juniper-Marinated Pigeon Breast with Radish Salad. (Photo courtesy of Janet Hutchings).

For the marinade
200ml/7fl oz good olive oil
10 juniper berries
1 sprig of thyme

1 sprig of rosemary
6 black peppercorns

For the sherry and balsamic dressing
1 teaspoon Dijon mustard
100ml/3½fl oz sherry vinegar
100ml/3½fl oz balsamic vinegar

500ml/18fl oz olive oil
30g/1oz caster sugar
Seasoning – salt and black pepper

Marinate the pigeon breasts in the mixture of the oil, juniper berries, thyme, rosemary and peppercorns for 48 hours. Dab dry and pan-fry for 3 minutes on each side. Take a hot pan, add the sugar and heat until it turns brown. Chop the figs in half and place flat side down. Deglaze with a little water.

Mix all the dressing ingredients together and shake well. Put the salad leaves into a mixing bowl, and lightly toss in the dressing. Thinly slice the radish and mix into the salad. Thinly slice the pigeon breasts and spread out on to the plate. Top with the salad, and serve!

Pigeon and Black Pudding Salad

Some people just do not like black pudding, but it works extremely well when accompanying pigeon – try it!

Pigeon and Black Pudding Salad.

100g/3½oz smoked bacon, cut into chunks
4 pigeon breasts
100g/3½oz black pudding, thickly sliced
100g/3½oz bag of supermarket mixed green salad

1 tablespoon of balsamic vinegar
2–3 tablespoons of olive oil
Salt and black pepper
Croûtons

Heat a little of the olive oil in a frying pan before adding the bacon; once the bacon fat has begun to run, add the pigeon breasts. In a second frying pan fry the black pudding slices, and cook the contents of both for 2 or 3 minutes on each side.

Once cooked, remove the pigeon, bacon and black pudding, but keep the pan in which the pigeon breasts have been cooked close to hand as you will need it again very shortly. Slice each breast into four or five pieces and crumble the black pudding, and add to the salad, tossing all together gently.

Add the vinegar and olive oil to the reserved warm pigeon pan in order to deglaze it; pour this dressing over the salad, and stir gently. Add the croûtons, and serve with crusty bread.

Roasted Breast of Pigeon, Black Pudding, Bacon, and Beetroot Glaze

The Boar's Head at Ripley near Harrogate, North Yorkshire, is a wonderful place to stay. Its food is also superb, and is served either in the restaurant (where paintings of people connected to nearby Ripley Castle look down benignly on the diner) or in the bistro, a charming and lively place much frequented by the locals. The castle has been in the hands of the Ingilby family for over 700 years. As the introduction to the guide book says:

> The history of the Ingilbys is a tale of romance, of courage in the face of adversity, of treachery and distinction. It is the story of how one family has survived everything that fate has thrown at them during almost 1,000 years. There is no concluding chapter because the family still lives at Ripley Castle, and today's events will be tomorrow's history.

The Boar's Head is also owned by the family and is presided over by general manager Steve Chesnutt and head chef Kevin Kindland. Kind by nature as well as name, Kevin gave us this pigeon recipe, which, as can be seen from others in this book, is a variation on the very popular theme of pigeon, salads and black pudding.

Olive oil
4 pigeons
1 garlic clove
3 sprigs fresh thyme
knob of butter

225g/8oz smoked bacon cut in strips
225g/8oz black pudding, diced
Beetroot glaze
Herb leaf salad
Aged balsamic vinegar

For the beetroot glaze
500ml/18fl oz beetroot juice
200g/7oz brown sugar

(cook and reduce until thick)

Roasted Breast of Pigeon, Black Pudding, Bacon, and Beetroot Glaze.

Heat the olive oil in an ovenproof frying pan. Place the pigeons, breast-side down, in the pan and brown all over. Add the garlic clove, thyme and butter. Turn the pigeons over and place in the preheated oven for 6 minutes, or until cooked pink.

Remove from the oven and leave to rest for 5 minutes before removing the breasts. Using the same pan, cook the bacon and black pudding – when cooked, set aside.

To present, place the herb leaf salad in the centre of the plate, and add a swipe of the beetroot glaze. Place the cooked bacon, black pudding and the pigeon breasts on the leaves. Finish by drizzling with aged balsamic vinegar.

RECIPES FOR PIGEON EGGS

Like most poultry, pigeons will continue to lay if the eggs are picked up and taken away, and worldwide, pigeon eggs are considered a great delicacy. In China, for example, they are hard-boiled and added to a great variety of Chinese dishes. Obtaining eggs might be more of a problem in the Western world, but we thought it might be interesting to include a couple of pigeon egg recipes, more in fun than for any real practical reason.

Pigeon Eggs with Black Pepper and Mushroom

This is apparently the 'classic' Chinese recipe for pigeon eggs; we believe it will serve four people.

12 pigeon eggs

A 'loose' 2–3 tablespoons olive oil

100g/3½oz small mushrooms (sliced if necessary)

100g/3½oz chicken meat, sliced and diced

¼ tablespoon minced (or 'Lazy') garlic

1 red pepper, washed, deseeded and very thinly sliced

For the sauce

6 tablespoons chicken stock

½ tablespoon of black pepper powder

½ tablespoon sugar and dark soy sauce

½ tablespoon light soy sauce

1 tablespoon cornflour

Hardboil the pigeon eggs; once they are cool, peel off the shells. Using two-thirds of the oil, quickly 'fry' the eggs in hot oil until they are golden in appearance; set to one side.

Use the remaining oil to stir-fry the mushrooms and chicken in a wok, then add the eggs, sauce and minced garlic. Mix together well. Dish up over a bed of rice, sprinkle the red pepper slices over, and serve immediately.

Curried Pigeon Eggs

If you have a ready supply of pigeon eggs and can be bothered to peel them after hardboiling, this makes a wonderful savoury starter – in the interests of research and authenticity, we've tried it! It serves four.

Curried pigeon eggs.

12–16 eggs, hardboiled
30g/1oz butter
1 onion, skinned and chopped
2 teaspoons curry powder
30g/1oz flour

250ml/8fl oz milk
55g/2oz sultanas
55g/2oz cucumber, finely cubed
Salt and freshly ground black pepper
225g/8oz long-grained rice

Boil the eggs, peel and keep warm in an ovenproof dish until required.

Melt the butter in a saucepan and fry the onion until soft, stir in the curry powder and flour, and cook gently for 1 minute. Remove the pan from the heat and gradually stir in the milk.

Bring back to the boil slowly and continue to cook, stirring all the while, until the sauce has thickened. Stir in the sultanas, cucumber and seasoning.

Cook the rice as per the manufacturer's instructions. Arrange around the pigeon eggs, and pour the curry sauce over.

Stuffings and Accompaniments

Most of our pigeon recipes are relatively simple to make and yet they are creative and imaginative – so much so that, with a little guidance and encouragement, there is no real excuse why almost everyone should not become an excellent pigeon cook. With just a few exceptions (mainly as a result of the kindness of professional chefs and restaurant owners), the recipes are made without any need to resort to unusual or difficult ingredients that would be out of place in an ordinary home. But (and it is a very big 'but') every single one of them will taste all the better for being accompanied by some carefully considered, and complementary, side dishes, sauces and pickles.

Imagination is important when it comes to accompaniments. Just think of where, and on what, a wild pigeon has been living, and try to ensure that the supporting vegetables, sauces and relishes around the plate reflect this. In the summer, for example, some new potatoes, freshly cut lettuce and leaves of wild rocket could form a base on which a lightly grilled pigeon breast is laid; whereas in the autumn, a whole pigeon could be slowly casseroled with wild mushrooms and pears from the orchard, and accompanied by freshly pulled carrots and lean, bright garden peas. Add a sweet chestnut stuffing to a whole roast pigeon in the winter, and your dinner guests will never want to leave!

STUFFINGS

With poultry intended for roasting it is far better to stuff them from the neck end, but with pigeons this is not really practical due to their small size. Therefore push as much stuffing as possible into the body cavity, and bake any remaining in a dish in the oven to use as a further accompaniment. Don't forget that any stuffing placed in the pigeon itself will marginally increase cooking times – and it's always worth brushing the breasts with a good coating of melted butter to ensure that the meat doesn't dry out.

Pan-fried or roasted, it is always worth ensuring that birds are coated in oil or butter in order that the meat remains moist.

Cranberry Stuffing

Cranberry stuffing goes particularly well with pigeon.

1 small onion, finely chopped
30g/1oz butter
175g/6oz freshly grated brown
   breadcrumbs
115g/4oz cranberries

1 tablespoon chopped parsley
¼ teaspoon ground mixed spice
Salt and pepper
1 beaten egg

First, sweat the onion in the butter. Once the onion has softened, stir in the freshly grated brown breadcrumbs, the cranberries, chopped parsley and mixed spice. Season with salt and pepper, bind the whole together with the egg, and leave to cool before stuffing the bird in the usual way.

Apple and Herb Stuffing

1 small onion, finely chopped
30g/1oz butter
1 large cooking apple, peeled, cored and
  chopped
55g/2oz fresh white breadcrumbs

1 tablespoon each of chopped parsley and
  thyme
Grated zest of a lemon
Salt and pepper
1 beaten egg

Sweat the onion in the butter until soft. Remove from the heat, allow to cool, and then stir in the chopped cooking apple, breadcrumbs, parsley and thyme and the grated lemon zest; season with salt and pepper. Bind all together with the egg, and leave until completely cold.

Lemon and Mushroom Stuffing

115g/4oz sliced button mushrooms
2 peeled and chopped shallots
4 tablespoons of white wine vinegar

The grated zest and juice of a lemon
About 6 sprigs of parsley and thyme
Salt and black pepper

Strip the leaves from the stalks of the parsley and thyme, then combine all the ingredients in a bowl; season with salt and black pepper. Stuff the pigeon and roast in the normal way.

Spinach and Mushroom Stuffing

Try this recipe with pigeon – it can be used to stuff a bird in the traditional way, or it can be finished under the grill and served as an accompaniment to the finished meal.

1 large onion, chopped
2 tablespoons olive oil
140g/5oz mushrooms
225g/8oz young spinach leaves

115g/4oz freshly grated breadcrumbs
100g/3½oz Cheddar cheese
Salt and pepper to season

Heat one tablespoon of oil in a heavy-bottomed pan and add the chopped onion. Cover and cook for about 15 minutes or until the onion is soft. Having roughly sliced the mushrooms – and be as adventurous as you like with whatever types are available from the greengrocers (unless you are absolutely positive of a correct identification, it is dangerous to risk using anything picked from the wild) – add them to the onion base, and fry them for 2–3 minutes. Then add the spinach leaves and cook only until they begin to wilt. Add the freshly grated breadcrumbs, season and mix well.

   Heat the remainder of the oil in a small non-stick frying pan and put the stuffing mix into this, pressing it down firmly (use a wooden spoon) so that the mixture forms a thick pancake. Fry the underside until it is crisp and golden coloured.

Spinach and Mushroom Stuffing – in the pan and ready to serve.

Remove from the hob and grate a thin layer of cheese over the top, then place the pan under the grill for a few minutes in order to brown off the top. Turn out on to a plate, and cut into wedges.

VEGETABLES

Because most game dishes are in season during the winter months, it makes sense to accompany them with a selection of winter vegetables. Swedes, carrots and parsnips are an easy choice, but what about a few winter greens? Broccoli served 'al dente' adds some vibrant colour, as does home-grown cabbage. Peas are, however (to our mind at least), the absolute saviour, and bearing in mind the fact that pigeon can be obtained all the year round, add a 'lift' to a winter meal when served hot and also to a summer salad when blanched and then served cold over freshly picked leaves and herbs from the garden.

It is all too easy to concentrate on the main course, and then at the last minute, panic about what can be served with it. To avoid falling into the trap of unimaginative accompaniments, try to consider the origins of subsidiary ingredients; an Italian-based recipe, for example, might suggest the inclusion of mixed fungi as a result of an autumnal walk in the countryside, whereas a Greek dish would just beg for a side dish of stuffed tomatoes

Winter-roasted vegetables, the perfect accompaniment to many pigeon dishes.

and olives. In Britain, one can have the best of all worlds: a light summer supper of pigeon breasts wants for very little in the way of an accompaniment; a winter stew of old birds can include all the root vegetables available in the casserole dish; and young birds roasted need nothing more than a tray of oven-roasted vegetables – easy to do and extremely tasty to eat!

Cheesy Salsify

Salsify was very much in vogue in Victorian times, and then went somewhat out of fashion. However, you can buy it in many supermarkets and speciality stores during the winter months, and it's also possible to buy it canned. When using it fresh, use roots that are well developed and firm to the touch. Cut off the root endings and then use a peeler to remove the outer skin and coating. To avoid discoloration of the root prior to its use, drop it into a solution of water and lemon juice.

750g/1lb 10oz salsify, prepared as above
   and cut into 10cm/4in lengths
150ml/5fl oz milk
150ml/5fl oz single cream
1 heaped tablespoon flour

¼ teaspoon grated nutmeg
30g/1oz butter
Salt and pepper
55g/2oz grated Parmesan
1 tablespoon chopped chives

Simmer the salsify in boiling water for 5 minutes; drain and place in a baking dish. In a saucepan, whisk together the milk, cream, nutmeg and flour with a fork, and begin to heat gently; add the butter.

Once the mixture has boiled and begun to thicken, season and stir in the cheese and chives; then pour over the salsify. Bake in the oven at gas mark 6/180°C for about 10 minutes.

Chickpeas with Spinach, Raisins and Pine Nuts

The Olive Oil Book by Louise Pickford (Salamander Books, 1994) has some very interesting vegetable dishes. Salamander is an imprint of Anova Books, London.

Serves 6–8
100ml/3½fl oz olive oil
1 small onion, sliced
1 clove garlic, chopped
450g/1lb potatoes, peeled and cubed
2 teaspoons cumin seeds, lightly crushed
2 teaspoons paprika
1 teaspoon chilli powder
400g/15oz canned chickpeas

150ml/5fl oz vegetable stock
450g/1lb fresh spinach leaves
55g/2oz raisins
Pinch of grated nutmeg
Salt and pepper
Juice of half a lemon
40g/1½oz pine nuts, toasted
Extra virgin olive oil, to drizzle

Heat 60ml/2fl oz of the oil in a non-stick pan, and fry the onion and garlic for 5 minutes until softened. Add the potatoes and spices, and fry for 10 minutes until golden. Add the chickpeas, their liquid and the vegetable stock. Cover and simmer for 10 minutes until the potatoes are cooked.

Meanwhile trim and wash the spinach and roughly shred. Heat the remaining oil in a large pan. Stir-fry the spinach for 3–4 minutes until just wilted. Stir into the potato mixture with the raisins, and cook for 2 minutes. Season with the nutmeg and some salt and pepper, and squeeze over a little lemon juice. Top with the pine nuts, drizzle over some extra oil, if wished, and serve.

Mushroom Casserole

Simple and easy – a mushroom casserole is a good companion to many pigeon dishes.

1 large onion, chopped	450g/1lb frozen peas
30g/1oz butter	Salt and pepper
450g/1lb mushrooms, wiped and sliced	750g/1lb 10oz cooked brown rice

In a large frying pan, sauté the onion in the butter until golden. Remove from the hob and add the mushrooms and peas, mix together well and season to taste. In a greased casserole dish, put alternate layers of rice and mixed vegetables. Place in an oven at gas mark 6/200°C and cook for 20–30 minutes.

OVEN-ROASTED CHIPS OF WINTER ROOTS

In their *Game and Cheese Book*, Alison and Stephen Morrell and Malcolm Pearce (*see also* the recipe for 'Pigeon Breasts with Lemon and Honey', page 40) suggest this interesting use of root vegetables – which will make the perfect accompaniment to many pigeon recipes. Thanks to all three for allowing us to reproduce it here.

Cut the vegetables into strips, some ten centimetres long and about half a centimetre wide. You can use a mixture of parsnips, swede, fennel bulbs, carrots and celeriac. When cooked the strips lose volume so allow sufficient for each person. Place the strips of vegetables in a large flat-bottomed roasting tray. Cover them with about three tablespoons of olive oil and grind over a little salt and black pepper. Toss the strips to make sure they are all well covered and move them around so that there is a single layer of vegetables only. Roast them in a very hot oven at gas mark 9/240°C for about eight to ten minutes and then turn the strips and continue roasting for five to seven minutes until they are crisp.

ORANGE MASHED POTATO

We were particularly taken with another of the vegetable recipes that appears in the *Game and Cheese Book*. We'd not considered the combination before, but as the authors state: 'All game responds well to fruit flavours, and this is a twist on an old favourite.' They also suggest that one should use 'normal varieties of potatoes for mashing such as Marfona, Golden Wonder or Maris Piper'. Boil the potatoes in the usual fashion.

> Work on the proportions of half an orange for each 400 grams (14oz) of potato. Drop the grated orange zest into the cooking water for a minute or two at the end just to soften it. Drain the potatoes and orange zest and then add the juice. Add about 60 grams (2¼oz) of butter and mash as usual making sure that the orange zest is equally spread through the potato.
>
> Of course, any not eaten immediately can be left to cool and then made into small 'patties' or potato cakes in your hands. If you wish, you can dip them in milk and sprinkle a little flour over them before frying them quickly in butter.

Jersey New Potatoes with Onions and Olive Oil

Elsewhere we have suggested using these as an accompaniment to *Pigeon Breast with Pineapple and Almonds*, but there's no reason why they shouldn't be used alongside a multitude of other recipes featured within these pages.

1kg/2¼lb Jersey new potatoes
4 onions, peeled and roughly chopped
2 garlic cloves, pushed through a garlic press
   (or use a little 'Lazy Garlic')

100ml/3½fl oz olive oil
1 bunch flat-leaved parsley, chopped and
   with any stalks removed
Sea salt and black pepper to season

Boil the new potatoes in the normal way – remembering that because they are small, they should only need about 10 minutes, or less – drain, allow to cool slightly and then cut them into quarters or, if really small, halves. In a large frying pan, sauté the onions and garlic in olive oil for about 5 minutes or until the onions are soft and shiny (not crisp and brown!). Add the chopped parsley and season with freshly ground salt and pepper. Add the potatoes, shake, toss or stir and when thoroughly heated through, turn into a serving bowl and take immediately to the table.

Pink Peppercorn Carrots

Many people believe that raw vegetables are much better for you than cooked, and it is true that if you boil vegetables you will lose much of their vitamin C, which is water soluble and sensitive to heat. But cooking can also increase the availability of some other ingredients: when carrots are cooked, for example, the cell membranes are softened, thus making beta carotene more available to the body. And yes, there is truth in the old wives' tale that carrots can help you see in the dark – well, perhaps not exactly, but it is known that beta carotene, together with vitamin C, can help in reducing the risk of cataracts!

450g/1lb carrots, topped, tailed and thinly peeled
30g/1oz salted butter (if you can get the
    French variety that contains little grains of
    sea salt, so much the better)

1 tablespoon pink peppercorns

Chop the carrots in half lengthways, and then into chunky julienne-type strips. Steam (or boil) until tender but not soft, and place in a serving dish. Add the butter and gently toss with a spoon until it has melted and the carrots are well coated. Sprinkle the peppercorns over, and take to the table.

Twice-Cooked Carrots

The addition of a little sugar to the water of carrots as they boil imparts an extra degree of 'sweetness' to their taste. Here the method of cooking is very different and the inclusion of a little sugar serves to form a sweet 'caramel'-type coating.

700g/1½lb young carrots, washed
    but not scraped
125ml/4fl oz olive oil
2 teaspoons light brown sugar

Salt and pepper
250ml/8fl oz white wine
1 teaspoon lemon juice

First cook the carrots whole and in boiling water until they are cooked. Allow to cool and then, as soon as you are able to hold them, slice them thinly. In a frying pan, heat the oil and then add the carrots. Spread the sugar over, season, add half the wine and the lemon juice, and simmer over a low heat.

Once the underside of the carrots begins to brown, turn them over, add the remaining liquid and cook until the slices are completely tender and the pan almost devoid of liquid.

Broad Beans and Parsley

In France, several decades ago, a certain Edouard de Pomaine wrote a little book in which he professed to be able to cook many meals in 10 minutes armed with not much more than a gas stove, a frying pan and a couple of saucepans. Delightfully written, the book's full title was *Cooking in Ten Minutes – or the Adaptation to the Rhythm of our Time*: a charming subtitle that we doubt has ever sprung to the minds of any of today's 'celebrity' chefs!

M. de Pomaine did, it must be admitted, 'cheat' a little by using tinned peas or tinned beans, and creating potato dishes by roasting them in their jackets the day before so all he had to do was just warm them through whilst the rest of the main course was being prepared. The basic ideas are sound, though, and fresh or frozen peas and beans would work well – and might even meet with the author's approval!

450g/1lb fresh or frozen broad beans	1 large sprig fresh parsley: taken from the
55g/2oz butter	stem and roughly chopped

Boil the beans until tender. Drain them through a colander and put them back into the saucepan over the heat before adding the butter and stirring well (but carefully so as not to crush the beans). Add the chopped parsley (and a little salt if wished), stir again and serve immediately.

Note: Edouard de Pomaine's marvellous little book also suggests adding small 'lardons' of cooked ham to peas; minced garlic to haricot beans; and thickened cream to beetroot that has been oven-cooked, before then being sliced and fried in butter. As we've mentioned many times before, a little imagination goes a long way when it comes to thinking of simple variations for what could otherwise be somewhat bland vegetable dishes.

Cauliflower with Lemon

If you really need to cook vegetables in a hurry like M. de Pomaine (see the recipe above), there is always the microwave. When microwaving any vegetables, always err on the side of caution and underestimate their cooking times, as they will continue to cook for a few minutes after the microwave has finished.

700g/1½lb cauliflower florets	2 tablespoons lemon juice
removed from their stalks	Paprika, to finish

Put the cauliflower into a shallow microwaveable dish and pour over the lemon juice. Three-quarters cover with cling film and cook on 'high' for 10 minutes. Sprinkle with the paprika before serving.

Almond Flakes and Broccoli

Sometimes a traditional Sunday vegetable can be given that little subtle 'lift' by combining something slightly unusual – such as almonds, for instance. Because almonds are also included in some of the pigeon dishes, all should 'marry' together very well indeed.

1 head of broccoli (450g/1lb)	30g/1oz flaked almonds
broken into florets	1 tablespoon softened butter

Boil or steam the broccoli florets until they are tender but still retain their vibrant colour. Drain thoroughly and tip into a serving dish before tossing in the butter and sprinkling with almonds.

Red Cabbage and Apple

Red cabbage is often eaten with pigeon – for some reason it works very well with most types of game. The addition of apples and raisins makes what at first seems to be a boring vegetable that much more interesting and flavoursome.

30g/1oz butter
1 large shallot, peeled and sliced
1 red cabbage, finely sliced
1 large cooking apple, peeled, cored
    and chopped

100ml/3½fl oz red wine vinegar
15g/½oz raisins
150ml/5fl oz water
1 tablespoon brown sugar
Salt and pepper

Using a large saucepan, heat the butter and gently sweat the shallot. Add the apple and cabbage, cover and simmer for a few minutes, and then add the remainder of the ingredients list. Bring to the boil and then turn to simmer until the cabbage is tender to taste. Drain and serve.

Cauliflower Pasta

Although intended merely as an accompaniment, this is an incredibly filling dish so you might like to slightly reduce the quantities.

300g/10½oz spaghetti
1 cauliflower, broken into florets
60ml/2fl oz olive oil
2 garlic cloves, peeled and chopped

115g/4oz white breadcrumbs
50g/1¾oz chopped hazelnuts
50g/1¾oz raisins
1 tablespoon chopped chives

Cook the spaghetti as per the packer's instructions for 5 minutes. Add the cauliflower florets and cook for a further 5 minutes.

Whilst this is doing, heat the olive oil in a frying pan and stir-fry the garlic, breadcrumbs, hazelnuts, raisins and chives (about 3 or 4 minutes). Drain the pan containing the spaghetti and cauliflower. Add the fried garlic/breadcrumb mixture, and mix in well with a wooden spoon. Serve immediately.

Leeks and Brown Rice

You could, if you wished, substitute spring onions for the leeks, but if you do, take note of the fact that they should be very finely chopped indeed and, unlike the leeks, do not need sautéing first – instead, merely add them to the rice after cooking and before allowing it to stand for a few minutes on the cooker top.

175g/6oz brown rice	55g/2oz butter
600ml/1pt chicken or vegetable stock	6 small leeks, finely chopped

Cook the rice in the stock for 45 minutes (with the pan covered and the heat set very low). Sauté the leeks in the butter without browning, then stir in the rice (if all the moisture hasn't been absorbed, remove the lid and turn up the heat stirring all the time with a wooden spoon until it has). Leave to stand without heat for a few minutes before serving.

Risotto with Green Beans and Mushrooms

Rice would be a natural accompaniment to all kinds of fish, salads and curried game dishes, but it also makes a perfect foil for many kinds of pigeon dishes. There are various types, and the one known as Camargue rice has a slightly nutty flavour that goes particularly well with pigeon recipes. As its name suggests, it comes from the southern region of France, but is nowadays available in the UK. If you cannot find a source near you, try a substitute of mixed long-grain and wild rice instead.

This rich risotto makes an ideal accompaniment. Venetians or inhabitants of the Po Valley in Italy will argue for many hours about the relative merits of Carnaroli, Vialone or Arborio rice. Here we use Arborio and a game stock base with asparagus spears and mushrooms.

A good handful of fresh green beans	350g/12oz Arborio rice
1 small handful button mushrooms, washed and sliced	1.2ltr/2 pints game stock
	1 glass dry white wine
1 medium onion, finely chopped	1 fistful grated Reggio Parmagiano or
45g/1½oz butter	other hard Italian cheese

Prepare the beans and boil them for 3–5 minutes, depending on thickness. Remove from the pan whilst just cooked but firm. Lightly fry the sliced button mushrooms in oil until just golden. Set aside.

Take a heavy-based pan, not too big, and sauté the onion slowly in the butter until soft, but do not allow to brown. This will take 5–10 minutes and should not be hurried.

Now add the rice, allowing this to become coated in the butter, say 2 or 3 minutes. Again it must not brown, so ideally stay with the risotto and get your guests to come and talk to you in the kitchen.

Now pour in the glass of wine and allow this to evaporate on a low heat – this will take another few minutes. From this point, the risotto should cook for a further 18 minutes. Pour on one third of the stock and allow this to simmer away. Add the remaining stock gradually until at the end the whole amount is absorbed; however, the risotto should never be allowed to become dry.

At the end of the cooking time, pour off any surplus liquid, depending on how dry or moist you like your risotto. Stir in the green beans, mushrooms and grated cheese. Test for seasoning, although it probably won't need any. Cover and leave to rest for 2 minutes before serving.

Risotto with Green Beans and Mushrooms.

MAKING STOCK

Many of the recipes in *The Pigeon Cook* call for the use of either chicken or game-based stock. Stock making is not an exact science and quantities of liquids and varieties of ingredients can be altered to suit; therefore do not be afraid to adapt any of the suggestions that follow. One word of warning: do not substitute ground black pepper in place of peppercorns, as prolonged cooking can turn ground black pepper bitter.

Game Stock

This can be made from the fresh carcasses of game birds or pigeons from which the breasts have been removed for another recipe, or if you have had a couple of roast birds, the leftover carcasses could be used. Giblets can also be included, or if you have a regular supply of birds throughout the season, they can be made into a separate stock (see below). The ingredients are as follows:

2 raw pheasant carcasses	3 bay leaves
Half a garlic bulb, roughly crushed	3 sprigs each of fresh thyme, rosemary
34 sticks celery	and parsley
2 small leeks	4–5 black peppercorns
2 small onions	About 4.5ltr/8 pints cold water
2 medium-sized carrots	

Place the carcasses in a heavy-bottomed pan. Add the garlic bulb, the celery, leeks, onions and carrots, all of which should be roughly chopped. Also include the bay leaves and the thyme, rosemary and parsley. Add the peppercorns and cold water. Bring to the boil and simmer gently for about 4 hours, skimming off the fat as it appears.

Once the process is complete, empty the stock into storage containers through a fine sieve.

Giblet Stock

For a small quantity of giblet stock, place the necks, gizzards and hearts of two or three birds into a heavy-bottomed saucepan and cook, adding just enough olive oil to ensure that they are slightly browned but without burning.

Stir in 1ltr/1¾ pints of water and bring to the boil, removing any residue floating on the surface. Add an onion, a celery stalk and a carrot, all roughly chopped. Include a *bouquet garni* (see Glossary) and five black peppercorns, then simmer for about an hour. At the end of cooking, pass the stock through a sieve, allow to cool, and store in the fridge for up to a week, or in the freezer for two to three months.

SUMMER SALADS

Salads can be a good accompaniment to many pigeon recipes, so we thought it might be useful to include just five examples in order to start the reader's creative thoughts!

Classic Green Salad

Use any combination of the following ingredients to make a green salad, such as is so often seen in France, where pigeons appear on many rural recipes. Try including lettuce, chicory, endives, sorrel, garden cress, watercress, young spinach, chard; very young dandelion leaves (the older ones are too bitter unless stood in cold water overnight), nasturtium leaves; cucumber, celery, Chinese cabbage; the green tops of chives, spring onions and shallots. Herbs can include parsley, tarragon and chervil.

Wash all the ingredients and dry thoroughly, using a wire salad basket or salad spinner (I always keep my spinner in the fridge, as this is probably the best place to store prepared salad ingredients for the longest period of time). Shred the greens with your fingers, rather than cut them with a knife, as they tend to 'bruise' less this way.

The French insist that a wooden salad bowl is best, the inside of which should first be rubbed with a cut clove of garlic. Place any dressing at the bottom of the bowl before adding the salad ingredients, but *do not* toss them until immediately before serving, otherwise the leaves will begin to wilt. Traditionally, salad servers must be placed crossed and resting over the rim of the bowl.

HERB COLD POTATO SALAD

Make your own potato salad by boiling up new potatoes until cooked but not about to break into pieces. When cool, cut into chunks and place them into a bowl of dressing made up of olive oil, a little sea salt and freshly ground peppercorns, chopped herbs such as parsley, chives and tarragon, together with a teaspoon of white wine vinegar.

Artichoke and Fennel Salad

Slightly complicated to prepare, this salad is nevertheless well worth the effort – provided of course, that you like the taste of fennel! Like the 'Classic Green Salad' above, it is French in origin.

7 artichoke hearts	600ml/1 pint water
½ fennel bulb	4 dessertspoons olive oil
1 small onion, peeled and chopped	Juice of a lemon
1 *bouquet garni* sachet (or make your own by securely tying thyme, parsley and a bay leaf in a square of muslin)	Salt and pepper
	2 dessertspoons fresh, chopped parsley

To prepare the artichokes, break off the stalks and cut and trim the base of the hearts; cut these into eight pieces. Thinly slice the fennel bulb. Place the artichokes, fennel slices and chopped onion into a heavy pan; add the bouquet garni and water, and cook covered for a half hour before draining and leaving to cool.

Toss all the ingredients in a dressing made up of the olive oil and lemon juice, and serve the salad garnished with the chopped parsley.

Tomato, Pineapple and Celery Salad

The idea behind this is American, and we have included it simply to show how simple salad ingredients can be mixed and matched to any occasion. Serving individual salads inside a tomato rather than in a bowl or on a side plate could add that little 'extra' something when produced for a lunch or supper to which guests are invited.

4 beefsteak tomatoes
2 sticks celery, finely chopped
2 rings of pineapple, finely chopped

55g/2oz chopped walnuts
Mayonnaise*

Cut the tops off the tomatoes, and remove the pulp and seeds. Fill with the celery, pineapple and walnuts mixed with the mayonnaise.

*Note: If you'd like to make your own mayonnaise, try this classic recipe:

Mayonnaise

Traditionally, the best chefs always make their mayonnaise in a cool place, using cool ingredients and utensils, and stir with a silver spoon!

1 egg yolk
200ml/7fl oz olive oil

1 dessertspoon white wine vinegar
Salt and pepper to season

Place a carefully broken egg yolk into a small mixing bowl. Add the oil, drop by drop, stirring gently all the time (with or without a silver spoon!). When the sauce begins to thicken, stir in the vinegar and seasoning. Add more oil, drop by drop, until the mayonnaise thickens even more, after which time the remainder of the oil can be gently poured

Tomato, Pineapple and Celery Salad.

in – stirring always – until finished. If the mixture refuses to thicken, or even curdles, try breaking another egg yolk into another basin and stirring the errant mayo on to it slowly. Taste, and if it has lost some of its 'bite', carefully add a few extra drops of vinegar.

'Salade Épinard de Le Malineau'

Jeremy says of this recipe: 'We don't always live so well at Le Malineau, our home in the Loire Valley. Occasionally, however, it's good to push the boat out, and we use this salad either as a starter or sometimes with "Smothered Pigeon"' (*see* page 24).

225g/8oz fresh garden spinach leaves	3 tablespoons olive oil
Sea salt and freshly ground black pepper	225g/8oz fine *pâté de foie gras*
1 tablespoon sherry vinegar	1 small (very small!) truffle

Remove the spinach stalks and wash the leaves, then pat them dry with kitchen roll or a clean tea towel. Roll them (in much the same manner as a Cuban lady might roll cigar tobacco on her thigh!) and slice into 1cm/½in strips.

Make a dressing by combining a pinch of salt, a little pepper, the vinegar and oil in a bowl. Add the spinach and toss it gently, before dividing it between four small plates or side bowls.

Being as careful as possible, cut the *foie gras* into twelve very thin slices and arrange three down the centre of each of the four plates or dishes.

Finally, cut the truffle into twelve thin slices (or more economically, grate a shaving or two of it!) and place one on each slice of the *foie gras*.

'Salade Épinard de Le Malineau'.

Rice, Cucumber and Orange Salad.

Rice, Cucumber and Orange Salad

A rice and orange salad would complement the flavour of cold pigeon breasts and is perfect in the summer months – it is also simple to prepare!

For four people

225g/8oz long grain rice
2 oranges
Half a small cucumber

Seasoning
3 tablespoons French dressing

Boil the rice and allow to cool. Peel, segment and finely chop the oranges, carefully removing all the pith and stones. Take the cucumber and slice it in half lengthways, and with a teaspoon, scrape out and discard the seeds. Then cut it into cubes and mix together with the rice and the orange; season well, and add the French dressing. Mix again and chill for an hour before serving.

GARNISHES

A few aromatic herbs sprinkled here, an eye-catching sprig of watercress there, all make a difference when presenting a pigeon dish to the table and are well worth the effort. Appropriately enough, considering the likely feeding habits of wild pigeons, young turnip leaves can be used as a garnish over roasted vegetables as well as at the side of a serving plate. Wash the leaves well, and while they are still wet, fry them in a tablespoon of olive oil, together with a crushed clove of garlic. Once the leaves have wilted, sprinkle them with a tablespoon of water and cook gently until the water has evaporated.

Use wild rocket with a pigeon-based risotto, and as an alternative to game chips, garnish a dish with root vegetable crisps, available from many supermarkets.

When you are considering serving chutney alongside a salad dish accompanied by a little pigeon breast, a really peppery leaf from watercress, or what is considered by many to be the perfectly delightful taste of wild rocket, will enhance the flavour of both the main part of the meal and the chutney.

CHUTNEYS AND PICKLES

Pickles and chutneys – especially the sweeter, fruity ones – go very well with a variety of pigeon dishes. We have written a book containing over 100 pickles, chutneys and relishes (*Making Traditional and Modern Chutneys, Pickles and Relishes*, The Crowood Press, 2010), many of which would be perfect accompaniments to the main recipes contained within these pages, so we thought it might be useful to include five of them here.

Red Cabbage Pickle

This traditional pickle is known in almost all of Britain's regions, but it is a particular favourite when accompanying pigeon dishes.

2 red cabbages	1 tablespoon black peppercorns
85g/3oz salt	1 dessertspoon coriander seeds
600ml/1 pint red wine vinegar	Small piece fresh ginger
600ml/1 pint distilled malt vinegar	4 bay leaves
4 whole dried chillies	1 tablespoon juniper berries

Quarter the cabbages and remove the stem and core. Shred very finely and place in a bowl, sprinkling layers with salt, and leave for 24 hours.

Meanwhile put the vinegars into a pan and add all the spices with the exception of the bay leaves and junipers. Bring to the boil and then simmer for 5 minutes before placing to one side to cool.

Next day wash and drain the cabbage and pack into four jars with the bay leaves and juniper berries. Pour in the strained vinegar and tightly seal the lids.

Red Cabbage Pickle.

Elderberry Pickle

Apart from perhaps blackberries, there can be nothing more traditional and better suited to a book that includes recipes for wild pigeons that spend much of their time in the hedgerows where elderberries can be found. As with most pickles and chutneys, this particular recipe tastes better if you allow it to mature for a few weeks before eating it.

450g/1lb elderberries
1.3kg/2¾lb apples
100g/3½oz stoned prunes
55g/2oz sultanas
55g/2oz stem ginger

900ml/1½ pints white wine vinegar
550g/1lb 3oz dark brown sugar
2 teaspoons ground allspice
90ml/3fl oz ginger wine

Remove the elderberries from their stems, wash them lightly and dry well. Peel and core the apples and chop them into medium chunks. Chop the prunes into small chunks.

Place all the ingredients into a large, heavy-bottomed pan and cook until the sugar has dissolved, stirring all the time in order to prevent the sugar sticking to the bottom of the pan and burning. Bring the mixture to the boil and then simmer for an hour, stirring occasionally, until it has thickened.

Have some warm, well cleaned jam jars waiting, and pour or ladle the mixture into them. Seal at once with well fitting screw tops.

Walton Heath Blackberry Chutney

Another 'hedgerow' chutney that goes well with some pigeon recipes; this one is from Lynn Brodie, who lives near Walton Heath, Surrey – hence the name of this particular chutney.

750g/1lb 10oz onions
500ml/18fl oz cider vinegar
300ml/10fl oz malt vinegar
1kg/2¼lb blackberries
1kg/2¼lb dried, ready-to-eat apricots
450g/1lb tinned crushed pineapples
225g/8oz sultanas
6 level teaspoons salt

1kg/2¼lb jam sugar (which includes pectin)
1kg/2¼lb soft light brown sugar
1 tablespoon ground pickling spices
2 tablespoons ground ginger
½ teaspoon Cayenne pepper
400g/14oz tomato purée
½ teaspoon paprika

Simmer the chopped onions in both vinegars until softened and opaque. Add all the other ingredients and cook until the chutney is thick. Take care to stir it regularly, especially later in the process once it becomes thicker: every 10 minutes to prevent it catching in the pan and burning, then every 5 minutes as it really thickens.

Once the chutney has reached a thick consistency, ladle it into hot, sterilized jars and seal with sterile lids.

Plum, Pear and Carrot Chutney

Mary Hart, who gave us this recipe, says that this chutney is the nearest thing to Branston pickle that you can get without it actually *being* Branston pickle. As such, it is another recipe that 'marries' particularly well with pigeon.

1kg/2¼lb plums, quartered and stoned
750g/1lb 10oz pears, peeled, cored and diced
750g/1lb 10oz cooking apples, peeled, cored
    and diced
500g/1lb 2oz shallots, peeled and diced

500g/1lb 2oz carrots, peeled and diced
250g/9oz prunes, stoned and chopped
500g/1lb 2oz soft brown sugar
600ml/1 pint cider vinegar

For the spice bag
55g/2oz root ginger, scraped and diced
1 hot chilli, chopped

2 teaspoons mustard seeds
3 teaspoons black peppercorns

Place the spices in a muslin square and tie it tightly. Place this, and all the ingredients (except the carrots) into a pan and bring to the boil slowly, stirring occasionally. Simmer the mixture for about 1½ hours, then add the carrots; continue to cook until the mixture is thick.

Pot into warm, sterile jars, pack down well in order to remove any air bubbles, then seal and label them.

Plum, Pear and Carrot Chutney.

Gooseberry Chutney

Mary Hart says that the essential difference between a commercially produced chutney and one made in your own kitchen is that in the latter, you can taste and identify the actual fruit! Here's another recipe from Mary, which not only offers a solution of what to do with all the gooseberries in the garden once you have had your fill of gooseberry pie, but also goes well with roast pigeon.

1.5kg/3lb 5oz gooseberries, topped and tailed	2 teaspoons salt
225g/8oz onions, chopped	½ teaspoon Cayenne pepper
300ml/10fl oz water	½ teaspoon dried garlic flakes
500g/1lb 2oz white sugar	1 whole cinnamon stick
1 tablespoon ground ginger	600ml/1 pint white malt vinegar

Place the gooseberries in a preserving pan together with the chopped onions and water. Cook very gently until soft and pulpy. Stir in the sugar and spices, and add the vinegar, stirring gently all the time. Still stirring, turn the heat up until the mixture is almost, but not quite, boiling. Reduce the heat and simmer the mixture, cooking gently for about 2 hours, or until it is thick.

Remove the cinnamon stick, and pour into warm jars; seal, label and store for at least six weeks before eating.

The correct vegetable accompaniments are everything.

Wine and Drinks

Never forget to serve chilled water at the dinner table; the continental Europeans always do, and there are several reasons for so doing. Firstly, in hot countries there is always the need to keep hydrated. Secondly, meals with friends are usually a long, protracted affair and if all that was on offer was wine, guests would be legless before reaching the stage of dessert! Thirdly, the occasional sip of water cleanses the palette and leaves the taste buds receptive to whatever food and wine the host and hostess are likely to offer during each course. There is also a fourth reason to consider, and no matter where you live, it is an elementary one: some guests may be designated drivers, decided non-drinkers, or simply allergic to alcohol.

Yet another reason is the fact that, if you serve a chocolate-sauced dish, for example, to non-drinkers and offered them a sweet, sickly fruit juice bought from the local super-market, their enjoyment of the meal would undoubtedly be impaired by the conflicting tastes. That is not to say that they should stick entirely to water, just that one should consider their needs.

Old-Fashioned Mint Lemonade

Non-alcoholic and perfect for summer pigeon dishes.

2.5ltr/4¼ pints water	75g/2¾ oz castor sugar
8 lemons, well and truly juiced!	1 large handful fresh mint leaves, roughly chopped

Place the mint leaves and sugar together in a bowl. Grind the two together until a paste is formed. In a kettle or large pan, boil the water before pouring over the mint and sugar mix. Add the lemon juice and leave to cool. Strain through a fine sieve and chill. When serving, serve in ornate glasses and garnish with slices of lemon and sprigs of very fresh mint.

HOW TO SERVE WINES

Most white wines do not require 'breathing' time, but red wines will. Malcolm Pearce writes in *The Easy Cook – Game and Cheese Book* that virtually all red wines will benefit from being opened a short time before being required – and he should know, as he has written many pieces for *Decanter* magazine and is a regular contributor to *France* maga-zine. Malcolm says that for the wine to be served *chambré* it does not have to be too warm: in the colder months, modern dwellings are generally kept at around 22°C, but this is too warm for red wines, and 16–18°C will suit them better.

If a wine is too cold, please don't put it in the hearth where one side of the glass will get really hot. People do regularly bring their wine to temperature by plunging it in boiling water, but what the true wine buffs think about that, we've no idea. It has been written on several occasions that wine, red or white, is best warmed by putting it in the microwave for 25 seconds. We've not put this to the test, nor will we probably ever do so.

On opening a bottle of wine, it is good practice (and a very enjoyable habit to get into) to pour yourself a small glass in order to test the appearance, scent and taste of the wine. This also has the advantage of increasing the area of wine in contact with the air; another way of doing this is to pour wine from the bottle and into a decanter. Make sure that the decanter is clean, though – there have been several cases of a good bottle of wine being lost because it has been poured into a decanter tainted with washing-up liquid or bleach. Should a decanter become stained and discoloured, it should be left overnight with water and denture cleaner in it, and then rinsed thoroughly.

WHAT WINE GOES WITH PIGEON

Woodpigeon breasts are more akin to grouse – at least to look at – and as such, you might suppose that they would benefit from being eaten alongside a heavy red wine. This would almost certainly be the case with a warming winter casserole, but if your pigeon is a reared one and therefore more like a little French *poussin* chicken, it would probably go better with a light red or even a white wine. Also, because pigeon is available all the year round and many of our recipes are served alongside light accompanying dishes such as salads, they too will most probably be best accompanied by a light wine. However, it is important not to get too hung up about your choice, and if you prefer to drink sparkling cava wine with everything, then don't feel ashamed about doing so.

Wines that should go well include the likes of French wines such as Savigny, Chambolle-Musigny, Crozes Hermitage and Nuits St Georges; an Italian Chianti Classico; a Californian Pinot Noir; and the Australian Majella. Much, of course, depends on the year as to its suitability – a long time ago, one of the authors bought several cases of 2003 Beaumes de Venise and fell in love with it as being brilliant for any occasion and with virtually any food. When stocks eventually ran dry, he bought, from the same Rhône vineyard, exactly the same wine made in 2005 and 2007: but pleasant thought it was, it bore no comparison to the 2003 – despite the fact that, in 2009, the 2007 had won the *Concours des Vins* gold medal.

Potted pigeon dishes or cold pigeon pie and terrines might be enhanced even further by being served with a white Burgundy, Cru Beaujolais, champagne or a good New Zealand chardonnay. We quite like the sparkling reds on such an occasion – look out for those made along the Saumur end of the Loire Valley. Rosés have their place and generally taste like white wine (they are made in the same way but from the skin of grape types more normally associated with reds). Oaky white wines go well with many autumnal foods, and some should therefore be perfect with many a pigeon dish.

Wine buffs will tell you that most South African wines are pleasant and fruity – so they, too, will go well with pigeon dishes – and comment on the fact that the wines of

Stellenbosch, Paarl and Franschhoek are on a par with their antipodean rivals. However, in keeping with the idea of locally sourced pigeon and accompanying vegetables from the garden, why not consider trying an English wine, rather than one from abroad? Although wine making in the UK has been practised since the Norman invasion, it was not until the 1980s and 1990s that the number of vineyards really increased and the production of wine was taken seriously. Now that it is, there are some extremely good wines to be had. Surrey, Sussex, Hampshire, Kent, Essex and the West Country are the most likely places to find vineyards – unsurprisingly, given the fact that they enjoy the climate most suitable for wine growing.

For a light summer lunchtime drink to go with a pigeon salad, you can do no better than try a country wine such as elderflower. Easy to make, all you need are the flower florets (how many depends on the strength of flavour you like in your wine), boiling water, dried yeast, a quantity of sugar and assorted fermentation jars, bottles, a funnel, some tubing with which to siphon off the wine, a plastic bucket with a lid – and the patience to wait a year whilst it matures.

BUYING WINE

You can, of course, just nip down to your local supermarket and buy some very good wines that are ready to drink along with this evening's chosen pigeon dish. They will be cheap and perfectly acceptable provided you have chosen a type that compliments any particular recipe – but why not consider buying wines to keep and let mature? There are several reasons for doing so, the first and most sensible being that, whilst good quality mature wines can be bought, they are generally quite expensive, whereas if you buy the same wine not long after it has been bottled and is first released on to the market (en primeur) about eighteen months later, it can be obtained at a fraction of the price.

When you are buying wines to keep, you need to look out for certain points, and the best place to do so is at a specialist wine merchant. If you pick the right one and tell them exactly what you are looking for (and, most importantly, how much you can afford to spend), they will be only too pleased to guide you through the process. Who knows, they might even have a few bottles opened and let you 'try before you buy'.

Once you've gained a little experience, you might consider buying your wine online or by mail order: it might even be worthwhile becoming a member of a wine club. Wine clubs (their brochures are often tucked alongside all the other advertising hype that normally comes with the weekend newspaper!) are a good way of trying the many different wine types, and once you've come across something you know you like and that goes well with your favourite pigeon recipe, you can seek out a supplier and buy a couple of cases.

TIPS FOR STORAGE

Many kitchen designers nowadays include a wine rack as part of the fixtures and fittings; however, the kitchen is not necessarily the best place to keep wine because it could be too warm and light. If you must store your bottles in the kitchen, remember that warm air rises, so put bottles of red wine at the top of your rack and the whites at the bottom where it is cooler.

The ideal temperature for storing wine (not serving it, which is a totally different matter) is anywhere between 6–14°C, and if you want to get technical, should have a humidity rating of between 55 and 75 per cent – so keep it well away from your central-heating boiler! Also avoid storing it in the utility room next to the washing machine or tumble dryer, because the vibration these machines cause will continually stir up any sediment. In an ordinary house devoid of cellars and *sommeliers*, the cupboard under the stairs is probably the best bet.

The Domestic Pigeon

It is, we think, worth including a few notes on the domestic pigeon due to the fact that, because some of the 'utility' breeds are slightly larger in size and heavier in weight than a woodpigeon, it is possible to use some of the bigger ones in the same way as one might *poussins* – the very young chicken so loved in French cooking. As a point of interest, we must point out that although we talk of 'domestic' pigeon, it is simply a term to describe reared birds (sometimes on a commercial basis), and most certainly does not include those dirty-looking, scrawny and often disease-ridden birds that frequent town centres, city parks and railway stations! There is, however, the well known story that when the novelist Ernest Hemingway was too poor to feed his family whilst living in Paris, he killed feral pigeons in the Luxembourg Gardens and took them home to eat concealed in his son's pram!

A BIT OF HISTORY

Domestic pigeons were once very popular as a source of meat throughout the whole of Europe, as they could, with the minimum of care, seek out most of their own food as they free-ranged over the fields immediately surrounding their purpose-built pigeon loft or dovecote. In certain parts of the UK, dovecotes were also incorporated into barns and other farm buildings – there is a fine example of this at the Weald and Downland museum at Singleton, West Sussex – even though it was far more common for such incorporated lofts to be included in northern outbuildings than it was in those in the south of the country. In the southern and eastern counties, brick and weather-boarded buildings looking a little like granaries were built as dovecotes, and the birds entered by means of a louvred affair situated in the peak of the roof.

As well as medieval manor houses where stone-constructed circular pigeon lofts could contain several hundred birds – which were, by that time, being kept intensively – many of the monasteries also included pigeon- and dovecotes to ensure that there was always a ready supply of fresh meat no matter what the time of year. Typical examples still in existence today show quite clearly the niches built into the wall, on which the birds would lay their eggs and rear their squabs. A long ladder that could be moved around the circular walls from a central point provided accessibility to all the ledges by the loft-keeper, who was often employed full-time to feed and otherwise take care of the pigeons in his charge.

In France, before the Revolution, it was only ever possible to have one of these build-ings (known as *pigeonniers*) having gained the express permission of the king and therefore,

The exterior of an ancient French pigeonnier . . .

. . . and the interior.

An ancient pigeon cote in northern Britain.

For a long time, some British houses had pigeon cotes attached to their houses.

Morocco, Egypt and several Asian countries use a traditional tagine to cook reared pigeon.

the only people able to put pigeon meat on to their dining table were members of the aristocracy – as a consequence of which, *pigeonniers* were as much a status symbol of their time as would be a Rolls Royce or similar model of car today. After the Revolution, however, it was most certainly 'power to the people', and under the new regime, every-one kept pigeons as a source of cheap, readily available meat.

SQUABS AND ADULT BIRDS

Modern day usage of very young pigeons in cooking is prevalent in North America, where many squab farms supply *haute cuisine* restaurants and the catering trade. Historically, the term 'squab' used to include the meat of all dove and pigeon species, however now it refers only to those birds bred specifically for the table. Commercial squab meat is tender and takes only half as long to cook as the meat from adult birds. It is also moist and richer in taste than many chicken dishes, which can be quite bland. In France it is often used in dishes that deliberately and carefully complement some of the country's most expensive wines; whilst in Chinese cooking, squabs are used in the creation of recipes traditionally used in annual celebratory events. Elsewhere – in Morocco, Egypt and several Asian countries for example – squab breasts stuffed with rice and herbs are a part of everyday cooking. It is, without a doubt, a most versatile meat, but is nevertheless spurned by many people on account of the very young age of the birds, the eating of which does not, for some reason, seem 'quite right'. Using adult pigeons in recipes is somehow more 'acceptable' – even though the meat from such birds is not likely to be as tender and simple to cook.

OBTAINING DOMESTIC PIGEONS

More so in Europe than in the UK, young, freshly dressed pigeons are, nevertheless, sometimes available at weekly/farmers' markets, and can be used for almost any recipe and cooked by any method. It should also be possible to buy reared birds from your High Street butcher (he may well have woodpigeon available in season, but if you particularly want the larger reared variety, it is important to tell him exactly what you're after). It is also always worth exploring the riches that may lurk in the hidden corners of the meat and freezer sections of your local supermarket.

Alternatively look online for suppliers: it seems that there are many in America, where commercial pigeon meat production is far more common than it is in the UK, but it is still possible to locate companies who can help you in your search. Not only are entire birds available by this method, so too are packs of breasts – an economical alternative considering the fact that you are only paying for actual meat, rather than a mixture of meat and obviously inedible bone.

KEEPING UTILITY PIGEONS

Of course, if you are a real pigeon-eating enthusiast, you would 'grow' your own and build a pigeon loft in which could be bred a regular supply of young birds, which would then obviously be readily available throughout a good proportion of the year. Pigeons bred specifically for the table are known as 'utility' types and include breeds such as the Cumulet, Carneaux, Utility King, Runt, Strasser and, in the USA, Texan Pioneers. Whilst all pigeons are edible, birds bred specifically for the table are typically much larger than those intended for racing or exhibition: the Runt (sometimes known as the Roman) can weigh as much as 1.5–2.25kg/3–5lb as opposed to the average 400–500g/14–17½oz weight of a racing bird.

The detailed construction of a loft and the breeding and feeding routines of domestic pigeon keeping are obviously outside the remit of this particular book title, but as pigeon keeping is possibly an idea worthy of consideration for the would-be smallholder, we have decided to include a very brief résumé of what might be required.

Housing
During the course of researching for this book, we have discovered that technically, only racing pigeons live in 'lofts'; exhibition pigeons are kept in 'coops', and table or utility pigeon types are housed in 'pens'.

Well designed housing should be secure from predators (including the family cat), be dry and airy (dampness and poor ventilation bring disease), and include nestboxes and perches. The actual size of the house will, of course, depend on the number of breeding birds one intends to keep. Unlike chickens and aviary birds, pigeons do not like conventional round perches, preferring instead either small square shelves (like the 'pigeon holes' often found behind the reception desk of an office or hotel) or inverted 'V'-shaped affairs. Nests are usually specially made terracotta or (more usual these days) plastic bowls lined with bought pads, wood shavings, shredded paper or, if there is a ready supply, dried pine needles. As pigeons often lay a second batch of eggs when the first set of youngsters are only a fortnight or three weeks old (and therefore still in the nest), you may need twice the amount of nesting pans.

Feeding

Commercially produced and packaged pigeon feed is easy enough to come by – just ask at your nearest agricultural suppliers or at any of the more traditional pet shops. Be sure to stipulate exactly the stage of growth of the pigeons you are intending to feed, as the nutritional requirements will vary depending upon the individual bird's development. Breeding adults will, for example, need a very different mix to squabs that have just been weaned and are heading for the table.

Some manufacturers of complete pelleted food maintain that grit is unnecessary as it is contained within the pellets' make-up, but otherwise all pigeons need a specialized mineral grit to aid digestion (general poultry grit should not be used for pigeons) and a ready access to fresh drinking water. Pigeons normally drink immediately after eating, and will drink far more when pellet fed than they will when being fed a more traditional grain-based mixture. Greenstuffs are also appreciated by pigeons of all ages.

Breeding

Provided that the cock-to-hen ratio is correct, pigeons can be pretty much left to their own devices when it comes to breeding, hatching and rearing their offspring; however, it is as well to remember that, for one reason or another, the eggs are not always fertile. If this is the case, let the adult pair try again – if they continue to produce infertile eggs then there is obviously something wrong, and they might be better culled from the flock. Birds are capable of breeding at six months, but most breeders agree that they should be nearer twelve months of age.

Pigeons usually lay two eggs, and both parents take turns in brooding them. When they hatch, the youngsters are quite often one male and one female (hence the expression 'pigeon pair'). In normal circumstances they are weaned at anywhere between twenty-eight and thirty-five days, and once you are sure that they are finding their own food rather than being fed by the parents (usually the cock bird at this stage), they can be moved to separate accommodation. To breed purely to produce squabs, however, they would be killed at about thirty-one days of age and should never need food provided by the breeder – in fact, it is considered that ten pairs of pigeon can produce eight squabs each month without them ever being fed anything other than the parents' pigeon 'milk'.

Sexing

It is not always easy to sex pigeons; experts suggest that it is a matter of experience rather than looking for any specific pointers. Generally males are a little larger (but you need male and female standing next to one another in order to compare!), but the biggest differences are in behavioural attitudes. Hens stand erect whilst cocks tend to strut and coo; and cocks drink by almost immersing their head in the water fountain and gulping, whilst hens are far more genteel and sip their water like Victorian ladies at a tea party. A mated pair shares the nest duties, cocks taking the mid-morning to early evening shift, whilst the hen broods for the remainder of the time.

Possible Disease Problems

Provided that they are well cared for, pigeons of any type are reasonably hardy – although as with all forms of bird, they can become infested by lice and mites if their pens are not kept clean and hygienic. As far as possible disease problems are concerned, the pigeon keeper needs to be aware of the symptoms of canker, coccidiosis and salmonella – and once these are diagnosed, the medications required.

Preparation for the Table

The preparation of domestic pigeons would follow the same methods as those used for woodpigeons (see Chapter 1), but it is considered that, in addition, they should be starved for twenty-four hours prior to killing. To avoid the meat from being any darker than necessary, once killed, birds should be bled whilst still warm before being plucked and drawn. Older birds may need more care in their cooking and are perhaps best used in recipes that require pot-roasting or slow cooking. In America and parts of Europe only potential breeding stock is allowed to survive longer than about four to five weeks before being killed for the table, and a pair of adult birds will, by this method, provide as many as fourteen or more eating squabs per season.

In Conclusion

So readily available if you are a woodpigeon shooting enthusiast living in the country, and relatively easily obtainable if you are not and have to rely on birds purchased from the game dealer or butcher, it is also possible, as we have just seen, to consider breeding one's own table birds for the future. The latter option might not be one for the squeamish, but unless you are a true vegetarian (and therefore unlikely to be reading this book!) it is important to remember that you are, by eating meat sourced from anywhere, indirectly responsible for the death of animals, fish and poultry that find their way into the human food chain – so what is the problem in producing your own? At least you can be sure that they have been looked after to the best of anyone's ability, and if an organically produced bird is important to you, on what they've been fed.

Once your mind is accepting of facts that we sometimes choose to ignore, the next step is to prepare pigeons in such a way that the maximum enjoyment is taken not only in their consumption, but also in their preparation – which includes understanding a little about how the bird is plucked, dressed and made ready for the table. Choosing a recipe can cause hours of mouth-watering anticipation and deliberation, whilst the correct accompanying vegetables, stuffings and sauces (and wine!) will ensure that whatever is chosen will indeed make a meal fit for any occasion.

If, as we have gone along, we have helped in making you want to be a pigeon cook, and as a result you earn the praise of your family and friends after serving a recipe from the pages of this book, then it has been worthwhile all round – you cannot believe the satisfaction we, as authors, gain from having someone say: 'We tried a recipe from one of your cook books the other evening – it was delicious!' As yet, no one has told us of any failures – perhaps they are being polite, or maybe it is because so many of the recipes have been kindly provided by enthusiastic chefs and cooks who fully understand the products with which they are working and have the imagination to 'marry' them to perfection.

ALL (AND MORE) YOU EVER WANTED TO KNOW ABOUT PIGEONS!

Finally, whilst entertaining your supper guests with one of the many superb recipes contained within these pages, you might like to regale them with a few lesser known pigeon facts – and so we list just a few of them here!

- To the Ancients, a white pigeon (or dove) was considered to be sacred, and was a symbol of the many gods that abounded at the time. It then entered Christian religion as a symbol of peace.
- In Turkey, in pre-Muslim times, it was believed that a person's soul was carried by pigeons to the gods.
- In the Middle Ages, pigeon guano was in such demand as a fertilizer that cotes were guarded in order to prevent it from being stolen. Another reason it was considered precious was because it contains saltpetre, an essential component of gunpowder.
- Pigeons have been used to carry messages in many wars, especially World War One where mobile lofts were set up behind the trenches from which the troops were fighting. They were, however, used long before that in peacetime, and the Ancient Greeks used pigeons to carry the results of sporting events. They were used during the Siege of Paris in 1870–71.
- The last official pigeon post service operated in India and was only disbanded in 2004.
- In the early seventeenth century there were around 26,000 pigeon houses in England – the inhabitants of which were kept to produce manure as much as meat.
- Pigeon droppings were an important part of the construction of gunpowder – it is perhaps no coincidence that, at Albury, Surrey, there was once a pigeon house that was home to over 600 breeding pairs of pigeon, and just down the road at Chilworth, there was a gunpowder factory that supplied Sir Francis Drake's battleships, among others.
- The names of pigeon breeds include delightful and mysterious ones such as Owl, Frill and Turbit; Archangels, Dragoons and the English Short-faced Tumbler (and the Long-faced Clean-legged Tumbler); Modenas, Magpies and Tipplers; Spanish Croppers, Barbs and Scanderoons – and that's just a few!
- As pigeons have monocular vision rather than binocular vision, they bob their heads up and down in order to gain a better depth of perception.
- Recent British kings and queens have all had lofts and been involved in pigeon racing – so much for the cloth cap image associated with pigeon racing!
- The boxer Mike Tyson has been a pigeon fancier all his life. In fact it is said that it was as a result of him protecting his pigeons from a local youth that he got into boxing. The story has it that the vandal wrung the neck of one of Tyson's birds; Tyson flew at the youth, flailing away with fists and feet until his tormenter fled, beaten and bruised. Someone witnessing the incident then persuaded Tyson to take up boxing training.
- Both the French revolutionary leader Maximilian Robespierre and the British librettist W. S. Gilbert (of Gilbert and Sullivan Fame) were life-long pigeon fanciers.
- Pigeons are considered to be amongst the most intelligent of birds, and are able to recognize all the letters of the alphabet.
- At Potters Field, just by the Lord Mayor of London's house, there is a huge statue of a common street pigeon. It was sculpted and designed with a toe missing, because so many street pigeons have suffered such a mishap due to the toe being accidentally 'amputated' by cotton thread left about the London streets and buildings.

Glossary

al dente Vegetables or, more commonly, pasta, cooked, but firm to the bite.

allspice Dried berry of the pimento tree of the clove family.

allumette Vegetables, potatoes or other items cut into the size and shape of matchsticks.

arroser To sprinkle with liquid, or to baste.

bain marie A deep container, half-filled with water in which other cooking pots are placed in order to cook gently in the oven. Usually used for terrines and similar dishes.

bard Place slices of bacon over the breast of pigeon to prevent it from drying out when roasting.

baste Regularly spoon over the roasting pigeon some of the fat or liquid in which it is cooking.

beurre manié A mixture, by equal parts of flour and butter, used to thicken sauces. *See also* roux.

black pepper Immature berries (white pepper is the mature berries with the hull removed).

blanch A cooking technique of placing food into boiling water for a short time, then in cold water to stop cooking.

bouillon Unclarified stock or broth from meat.

bouquet garni Sprig of thyme, parsley and bay leaf, tied together and used to flavour stews and casseroles.

braising A combination of roasting and stewing; usually used on tougher joints of meat.

broil Method of cooking to describe grilling a dish in the bottom of a grill pan when other ingredients and liquid mixes have been added.

cassoulet A casserole of stewed meat and beans.

Cayenne Powdered red pepper.

celeriac The root of a variety of celery, used raw or cooked in a variety of pigeon recipes.

chervil A mild, aniseed-flavoured herb related to parsley.

chilli peppers Many varieties from mild to hot.

clarified butter Butter cleared of impurities by melting slowly and removing the unwanted liquid that forms at the base.

concasser To chop roughly or pound in a mortar.

coriander seed Used whole or in coarse or fine powder form. This herb is of the carrot family and has the flavour of sage and lemon peel. When stocking your pantry get both the seeds and the powder.

croûton   Small cube of fried or toasted bread served as a garnish to soup or alongside certain pigeon dishes.

deglaze   To loosen meat residue in a pan or roasting dish after roasting or frying with a wooden spoon and adding wine or stock in order to make gravy.

dice   To cut food into small cubes of about 5mm (¼ in) across.

duxelle   A purée of very finely chopped mushrooms, sweated in butter, with a little chopped onion, which can then be used for stuffing pigeon, or as a sauce base.

earthenware   Cooking pot made of fired clay.

émonder   To skin tomatoes, peppers, by plunging them into boiling water for a few seconds and then dipping them into cold water.

étouffé   A cooking method similar to braising in which items are cooked with little or no added liquid in a pan with a tight-fitting lid.

farina   Flour or meal made of cereal, nuts, or starchy roots.

farrago   Medley or mixture of foodstuffs.

filo   (pastry) A type of leaved pastry.

fines herbes   A mixture of finely chopped herbs, traditionally chervil, chives, parsley and tarragon.

fumet   In cooking, the juices that have run from meat during cooking – elsewhere it is a name for deer droppings!

garnish   To decorate food dishes, especially just before serving.

glug   A glug (or two) of oil or wine is often referred to by modern chefs – although a very loose measurement, it is described thus: put your thumb over the top of the bottle and tip it up. When you let your thumb off, the liquid will glug once, or twice (as required) as it comes out.

gremolata   Very finely chopped lemon zest, juice and parsley.

infuse   To steep herbs or similar in liquid in order to extract the flavoursome content.

julienne   Vegetables cut into short thin strips.

larding   A method whereby thin strips of fat are pushed through meat in order to prevent it from drying out during cooking.

lardons   Small squares of bacon or pork belly fat (alternatively spelt as 'lardoons').

legumes   Any member of the pea family, including chick peas, runner beans, soya beans and lentils.

mandolin   Not in this instance a musical instrument, but a slicer used to produce julienne vegetables.

marinade   A liquid and/or herb mix in which meat and game is left for several hours. *See also* marinate.

marinate   To add liquid or dry (or a mixture of the two, such as wine and herbs) to meat or fish in order to impart flavour or to tenderize.

medallions   Small rounds of meat.

mirepoix   Coarsely diced vegetables.

mixed spice   Classically, a mixture containing caraway, allspice, coriander, cumin, nutmeg and ginger.

papillote   Greaseproof paper or kitchen foil forming a casing around food in order that meat can self-baste whilst roasting.

parboil To partially cook food by boiling briefly in water.

peppercorns Most often used whole. If required in powdered form, they taste best when freshly ground.

pinch An approximate measure of any ingredient, but usually an amount held between thumb and forefinger.

ragoût Meat stewed with vegetables and highly seasoned.

reduce To reduce a liquid-based mixture by boiling until it thickens to the right consistency.

refresh Most commonly used in reference to blanched vegetables that are placed immediately in iced water to stop the cooking, set the colour and restore the crispness. Greens and herbs that are still very fresh, but have gone limp, can be restored to their original state by placing in cold water and then patted dry.

roux A mixture of fat and flour used in sauces.

quenelles Technically, a lightly poached dumpling based on a mixture or combination of chicken and/or rabbit bound with eggs and shaped into an oval by the use of two spoons, but used generally to describe the method of serving mashed potatoes and/ or vegetables.

sauté Rapid cooking in oil, usually in a heavy-bottomed sauce or frying pan.

searing To quickly brown meat at a high temperature in order to retain its juices.

spice bag Home-made muslin bag used to hold spices in order that they might add flavour to a cooking dish without leaving a bitter taste.

suer *See sweat.*

sweat Cooking vegetables very slowly in butter or oil so as to draw out the moisture and soften them. Care must be taken that the fat does not become too hot and brown otherwise the vegetables will just remain raw and burn.

tagine An African cooking pot very useful in cooking certain casseroled pigeon recipes.

translucent Cooking (onions, for example), until clear or transparent.

trivet A metal rack placed over or in a roasting tin to keep the meat from sitting in its own juices.

trussing A method of holding game or meat together by tying with string and the aid of a skewer.

whisk Utensil for whisking, or the action of whipping or mixing eggs, cream, with a brisk sweeping movement. Usually necessary in recipes where air needs to be added, such as in the making of soufflés.

wine vinegar Vinegar made from wine as opposed to malt.

wood grilling By barbecuing over charcoal, the wood imparts a distinctive and unique flavour to the meat.

zest Scraping of orange, lemon or lime peel used as flavouring.

'At-a-Glance' List of Recipes

The following list is not in any alphabetical order (for that you will need to refer to the index), but more or less follows the recipes as they appear in the text. The idea behind its inclusion is simply so that you can run your finger down the list, decide what might tickle your particular fancy, and then refer to page details and the like via the index. The inclusion of a list like this has become a habit in all our books on cooking, and it is surprising how useful people seem to find it. Ideas for stuffings and accompaniments follow on directly after the list of main dishes.

Pigeon Pie
Smothered Pigeons
Roast Breast of Holkham
  Pigeon, Toasted
  Brioche, Rhubarb and
  Redcurrant Compôte
  with Black Peppercorn
  Ice Cream
Pigeon in Pears
Pigeon Hot-Pot Sausages
  with Pears
Roast Holkham Pigeon
  Breasts, Braised Puy
  Lentils, Lardons and
  Salsa Verde
Pigeon Bruschetta
Pigeon, Mushroom and
  Watercress Bap
Pigeons Saint Germain
Breast of Holkham Pigeon
  with Vietnamese
  Coleslaw

Pigeon Breasts with
  Cassis and Raspberries
Potted Smoked Pigeon
  with Duck Legs and
  Chicken Breast
Austrian Stuffed Pigeon
Pigeon Tikka
Pan-Fried Pigeon Breast
  with Creamed
  Potatoes, Celeriac and
  Rocket
Pan-Fried Woodpigeon,
  Celeriac Puree and
  Juniper Berries
Reared Pigeon with
  Honey Sauce
Pigeon Breasts with Lemon
  and Honey Sauce
Roast Woodpigeon with
  Potato and Beetroot
  Rosti, Calvelo Nero,
  Beetroot and Twice

-Cooked Jerusalem
  Artichoke
Roast Pigeons in a Bed of
  Garlic
Tipsy Pigeons
Russian Pigeon
Simple Ways with Young
  Pigeons
Braised Pigeon with
  Orange
Pigeon Breast with
  Pineapple and Almond
Pigeons à la Française
Barbecued Pigeon Pieces
  with Saffron and
  Yoghurt
Spanish-Style Pigeon
Grilled Pigeon
Quick and Easy Pigeon
  Cannelloni
Carpaccio of Essex
  Woodpigeon

Pigeon in Minutes
Pigeon Breasts in a Wild
   Mushroom Sauce
Roast Woodpigeon with
   Pickled Beetroot,
   Beetroot Purée and
   Horseradish Cream
Casserole of Pigeons
Pigeon Breasts and
   Sausage Stuffing
   'Sandwich'
Pigeon Enchiladas
Pigeon with Tomato and
   Chocolate Sauce

Pigeon 'Scampi'
Hungarian Pigeon Soup
   with Pickled Gherkins
   and Soured Cream
Stuffed Pigeon
Macbeth's Pigeon
Pigeons with Cherries in
   Eau-de-Vie
Mustard Grilled Pigeon
   with Poppy Seeds
Pigeon Stir-Fry
Pigeon Salad with Bacon
   and Blackberry
   Vinaigrette

Pigeon with Warmed
   Mushroom Salad
Juniper Marinated Pigeon
   Breast with Radish
   Salad
Pigeon and Black Pudding
   Salad
Roasted Breast of Pigeon
   Black Pudding, Bacon
   and Beetroot Glaze
Pigeon Eggs with
   Black Pepper and
   Mushroom
Curried Pigeon Eggs

STUFFINGS AND ACCOMPANIMENTS – AT A GLANCE

Cranberry Stuffing
Apple and Herb Stuffing
Lemon and Mushroom
   Stuffing
Spinach and Mushroom
   Stuffing
Cheesy Salsify
Chickpeas with Spinach,
   Raisins and Pine Nuts
Mushroom Casserole
Oven-roasted Chips of
   Winter Roots
Orange Mashed Potato
Jersey New Potatoes with
   Onions and Olive Oil

Pink Peppercorn
   Carrots
Twice-Cooked Carrots
Broad Beans and
   Parsley
Cauliflower with Lemon
Almond Flakes and
   Broccoli
Red Cabbage and Apple
Cauliflower Pasta
Leeks and Brown Rice
Risotto with Green
   Beans and Mushrooms
Game and Giblet Stock
Classic Green Salad

Herb Cold Potato Salad
Artichoke and Fennel
   Salad
Tomato, Pineapple and
   Celery Salad
Salade Épinard de Le
   Malineau
Rice, Cucumber and
   Orange Salad
Red Cabbage Pickle
Elderberry Pickle
Walton Heath
   Blackberry Chutney
Plum, Pear and Carrot
   Chutney

Index

Entries in *italics* denote actual recipes